THE ROAD TO
BELONGING

My Journey to Punta Gorda, Belize

By

Francis Mandewah

TELEMACHUS PRESS

THE ROAD TO BELONGING: MY JOURNEY TO PUNTA GORDA, BELIZE

Edited by: Jeannita D. Triggs, Ph. D.

Interior photographs property of Francis Mandewah unless otherwise noted.

Publishing services by Telemachus Press, LLC.
7652 Sawmill Road, Suite 304
Dublin, Ohio 43016

Visit the author website
https://www.francismandewah.com

ISBN: 978-1-965121-38-2 (eBook)
ISBN: 978-1-965121-39-9 (Paperback)

BIOGRAPHY & AUTOBIOGRAPHY / Memoirs

Version: 2025.10.27

This book is dedicated to the Punta Gorda branch of the National Garifuna Council of Belize.

Table of Contents

THE ROAD TO BELONGING

My Journey to Punta Gorda, Belize

Preface

FRANCIS MANDEWAH'S STORY began in a remote village in Sierra Leone, where the odds were stacked against him from the very start. Through an extraordinary twist of fate, Francis managed to receive a good education—a rare opportunity for a poor village boy. This chance set him on an epic journey that would take him far beyond anything he could have ever imagined.

Driven by faith and dreams bigger than his surroundings, Francis embarked on a perilous adventure that would eventually lead him to the United States. Along the way, he crossed the vast and unforgiving Sahara Desert, traveling in an open-air convoy—a feat few would dare attempt. His journey took him to Italy, where a new chapter began.

Francis captured every twist and turn of his remarkable journey to America in his adventure memoir: *Friendship: A True Story of Adventure, Goodwill, & Endurance*. [https://www.amazon.com/dp/1942899882]

Published in 2016 in the United States, the book chronicles his transformation from a young boy in Sierra Leone to a man attaining his cherished goal of living in the United States. The memoir has received an international Book Excellence Award for Memoir writing and has continued to receive five-star reviews on Amazon, Barnes & Noble, Goodreads, and in Europe at Waterstones Bookshops in London and Wales, as well as stores in Brussels, Berlin, Amsterdam, Rome, and Copenhagen.

Now, in his latest book, *The Road to Belonging: My Journey to Punta Gorda, Belize*, Francis reflects on a life-changing journey, an answer to a pull for something different—a longing for a new chapter that would reinvigorate his spirit. His path to and through America was never easy, but Francis's resilience and adventurous spirit saw him through every challenge. Upon retirement he finds himself asking: what's next? He chronicles the answer to that question and his pursuit of yet another goal: spending his retirement years along the coast of Central America.

For Francis, *The Road to Belonging* is not just the story of an adventure, it is a tale of discovery of unexpected connection and community. He shares his fascination and the joy of learning that he underwent searching for his new home in Belize, a place that he didn't know he was looking for until he found it. Assimilating into his new home was like being reborn. Like many true adventurers, he is constantly driven by a deeper yearning: one seeking a new perspective.

As you read this book, you will see how Francis brings Belize to life on its pages—shares its colors, rhythms, and spirit—while inviting you to walk alongside him on the road that led not only to a new country, but to a deeper sense of belonging.

Chapter 1

I OBSERVED AN older lady leaving a grocery store in South St. Louis, Missouri on a Tuesday afternoon. I guessed she was Cambodian. She seemed content enough, though struggling a tad. She carried with her 3 bags, filled to the brims with groceries. I was headed to a workshop on "Diversity in the International Community." I'd left my car at the park-and-ride lot one block back. The woman and I arrived at the traffic light at the same time. She seized the opportunity to set her load down for a moment while the light was red. One bag rested between her feet, another on her left hip, and the third hung heavily from her right hand. She seemed to have a firm grasp on her situation.

The intersection teemed with people. Busy day. The light changed and the crosswalk was clear. The crowd began to make its way across, but as the woman reached for the bag between her feet someone bumped her and the contents of the bag on her hip went spilling into the street. The pedestrian that bumped her seemed unaware of their effect, and other passersby simply stepped over her belongings and went about their way. I felt for the woman and knelt down to help her gather her belongings, the timer on the crosswalk quickly counting down. In the nick of time, we gathered her things. I saw that the fall had torn her reusable shopping bag.

The woman shook her head frantically and said, "No. No. No," grasping at air. She began saying something in a language that I did not understand. She looked around and seemed crestfallen, as if she didn't know what to do.

She began to whimper and murmur in what I assumed was her native tongue. I looked at my watch. I had less than an hour before my workshop began. I decided that if I hurried, I could help this woman find her way and still make it to class. I put my hand on the woman's shoulder and nodded my head "Yes." The woman raised her eyebrows, and I put my right hand over my heart and said, "Francis. My name is Francis." She smiled. "Bihn." She put her hand on her heart and repeated her name, "Bihn."

Before the light turned again, I helped her gather her bags, and we prepared for the walk. I followed her without hesitation. I cradled the busted bag in my left arm and carried another bag in my right hand. I minded my pace to accommodate her slow waddle. We exchanged smiles each time I looked over to check on her and repeatedly gestured for her to lead the way.

I wondered how such a small woman could carry such heavy bags. I wondered how often she did this. I stood on the southeast corner of Morganford and Gravois Roads next to Bihn wondering what our next steps would be. If she knew exactly where she was going or if she was, in fact, lost. When the #10 Gravois bus pulled in front of us, she stopped and stepped on. She jerked her chin up for me to step on also. I followed reluctantly. "What have I gotten myself into?" I asked silently. After ten minutes on the bus her mood seemed to lighten. I assumed that things began to look familiar to her. Her eyes lit up, and she shook her head "yes" and said the word aloud as she pulled the call string. She was waving me on, saying "Come."

Still carrying her bags, I followed the little woman off the bus and down the street. Now I definitely had no idea where I was. We walked for several blocks in a single direction. Where was she taking me? I had no intentions of following the woman far. I assumed she was only a few blocks away from home when I first spotted her. I didn't have time for this. I would be late for class, and my job would not approve of me being late for this required training workshop.

Bihn waddled at a steady pace, walking straight down the long street, finally making a left turn down a side street then dipping into an alley. She arrived at a brown door, mounted the stoop, and set her bag down. She reached inside her shirt and fished out a shoestring with two keys on the end of it. She used the larger key to open the big brown door then grabbed the handles of her bag once again and said to me once again, "Come." The hallway up the stairs was dark, narrow and murky with peeling green paint on the walls. At the top of the landing there were three doors, all brown with silver-colored locks. The carpet was clean, and the air smelled of pine scented cleaner.

She once again set her bag down and pulled out the string from her shirt. She used a golden key to open the door and moved forward, dragging her bag inside. "Come. Come," she said. I walked inside, sat the bags on a wooden table with a crisp white tablecloth and turned to leave. Just as I did, a young, black-haired man appeared in the doorway. He instantly took a fight stance and started shouting in English, "What are you doing? Who are you and why are you in my house? Get out." Bihn came and stood in front of me, guarding my body with hers, waving the young man off vigorously. She said something I couldn't understand in her native tongue.

"*Tôi xin lỗi,*" the young man said. I would find out later that his words meant "I'm sorry," in Vietnamese. "Thank you for seeing my grandmother home safely. Can I offer you something to eat?"

"No. I really must go," I said. "Have a good rest of your day. Be well."

The young man didn't know it, but his stance had been quite intimidating, and I left the apartment with my heart pounding. What if he'd been just a little bit more rash and Bihn had moved just a little bit more slowly? It could have ended ugly. I counted myself lucky and made my way back to the bus stop.

When I made it to the workshop the lecture was in full swing. Thankfully the moderator did not call me out for being late. The segment's topic was respecting and practicing diversity: what do we focus on in the practice of diversity? What does the practice of diversity look like? What does it sound like? Does diversity have a taste? I raised my hand and said, "The practice of diversity has a sound. The practice of diversity involves making an effort to communicate across language barriers. I speak five languages, but today I came in contact with an unfamiliar language. My challenge was to communicate with almost no words, because we did not share a common language. I could have refused to help because this woman didn't speak English, but I couldn't do that. My conscience wouldn't let me."

"Good. What else?" the moderator said, looking around the room. "Gender." "History." "Culture." "Economics." "Education." The ideas came pouring out from every corner of the room. All great foci. I looked around the room and recognized people from all over the globe. In that very classroom we had people from China, Southeast Asia, Africa and the United States.

I wondered about Bihn's life. Her culture and education and how she came to be in the United States. How long she'd been here and whether or not she was a citizen. I knew that God had chosen to work through me to help her that day, and I rested well that night having been His tool.

~~~~

I am an African immigrant whose journey to the United States began with a single act of kindness by a generous American pilot from Milaca, Minnesota, Tom Johnson. Tom rescued me from the poverty, physical abuse, and chaos of war-torn Sierra Leone. He didn't just change my life—he gave me the chance to rewrite it entirely, trading fear for freedom and despair for opportunity. I quickly realized that I could never repay his kindness, but I could prove myself worthy.

God has shined his light on my life. He has held my hand as I've tried to find a home for myself in America from Massachusetts to Wisconsin to Missouri. For 33 years, I played by the rules in America. I worked hard, followed the law, and chased my dreams with relentless determination. In 2015, I retired from the Wisconsin Department of Corrections. I had been so laser focused on work that I hadn't given much thought to where or how I would spend my retirement. Afterall, though I had more life behind me than in front of me, I was still young. What would life be like without a daily commute complete with rush hour gridlock on the Poplar Street bridge from Missouri to Illinois?

My gratitude for Tom Johnson, and for the opportunities America gave me, ran deep. Would America be my final destination, or could there be more world to explore? I was proud of my achievements—educational, professional, personal—and the life I had built. Yet, my journey had not been without hardship. Marital troubles tested my resilience, and my time working for the Wisconsin Department of Corrections brought its own set of challenges, both personal and professional. There has been more celebration than sorrow. What was missing from my story upon retirement was a home. I couldn't see myself remaining in Wisconsin until I was old and gray. What would I do? Where would I go? I recalled talking to my colleagues about the future. There were those who said they would move to be with their grandkids after retirement, or go play golf all the day long in Florida, or return to their hometowns and reconnect with the family and friends they grew up with. I have no grandchildren, no desire to play golf, no actual "hometown" to return to in Sierra Leone. Since Tom's death, I had no enduring connections anywhere in the United States. So, I was faced with two problems: Without an office to go to everyday, what would I do with my time? and where would I find "home" in my retirement years?

Instinctually, I found another job, deciding to work beyond retirement. I moved from Wisconsin to Missouri and worked for the Illinois Department of Corrections in East St. Louis. Before long, I began to feel trapped in a monotonous routine, performing the same tasks day after day without truly feeling alive. I couldn't see myself remaining in my upstairs, two-bedroom apartment in St. Louis, Missouri until I was old and gray. I found myself yearning for a new adventure—I longed to be somewhere far from the relentless pace and noise of American life.

I thought about returning to Sierra Leone. Over the years my sisters and I have nurtured our family connection. I'm in frequent contact with my sisters and nephews and nieces via cell phone, which enables me to call, speak to them with clarity, and actually see their faces and the people in my village in real time. Sierra Leone is still reeling from its war-torn era and is in some ways unsafe and underdeveloped. After so many years overseas, I would be considered a foreigner, and it would be especially unsafe for me. Additionally, the medical care in Sierra Leone does not compare to the advances in infrastructure and medicine in the United States. After much consideration, I concluded that, though I wanted to escape the rat race of American city living, returning to Sierra Leone was not really in the cards. Sierra Leone will always be my first home—the place where my mother's love shaped me. It is the place of my earliest memories.

My neighbor suggested that winter in the Midwest had given me cabin fever: I spent all of my time in doors: home to work; work to home; home to church; church to home; repeat. I prayed for a solution, prayed that my unease be soothed. One cold Saturday in November, in a fit of boredom, I decided to go thrifting. I enjoy sifting through the trinkets and books. There are always hidden treasures. I frequented thrift stores in my surrounding area. The Goodwill and St. Vincent de Paul's often carried new items that were generously donated by corporate sponsors. I, too, often donated items to these stores to help with their fundraising efforts, and whenever I was in the mood to fill an empty space on a shelf I'd head to the thrift store to find a trinket or a book to fill the space. Browsing through the Goodwill, I stumbled upon a book: *Lonely Planet: Central America*. Its pages were filled with pictures of lush green landscapes and the cool blue waters of the Caribbean Sea. I stopped at the chapter on Belize.

A light bulb switched on in my head. I recalled the vacation stories of one of my Wisconsin coworkers. His parents had gone on vacation in Belize and couldn't praise the place enough: "it was the perfect mix of traditional living and modern luxury." I stood there enraptured with the pictures of the mountains with their winding roads and the forest alive with colorful birds. Oh, and the people! The people in one of the pictures looked like me. I had to squint to convince myself that I wasn't looking at a picture of my own sister. I paid the $2.00 for the book and left Goodwill with my imagination ablaze.

Belize. The young Caribbean nation in Central America seemed to shimmer with promise. The more I learned, the more fascinated I became. I watched videos and read stories about Belize's vibrant tapestry of cultures: the Mestizo Yucatec Maya[1] in the north, the Mopan and Ketchki Q'eqchi Maya in the south, the Creoles in Belize City, the Garifuna in the South, the Mennonites in the northwest and south, and the East Indian communities along the southern coast. Each group had its own unique history, but it was the Garifuna people who captured my imagination most powerfully.

The colonial history of Belize is deeply intertwined with chattel slavery and the country's fight for emancipation. Africans were brought to Belize to cut mahogany and logwood, their labor forming the backbone of the settlement's economy. When Britain passed the Slavery Abolition Act in 1834, freedom was granted in name but delayed in practice. The "apprenticeship" system forced men and women to remain tied to their former masters for years before true liberty was realized. Many freed men and women settled in villages outside Belize Town, where they relied on subsistence farming, fishing, and small-scale trade to survive independent of the colonial elite. Out of this rebirth grew what we now recognize as Creole culture, central to Belize's language, music, food, and identity.

---

[1] Maya is the Western adjective form of Mayan

The Garifuna, also known as Garinagu, live primarily in Dangriga, Hopkins, and Punta Gorda and are descendants of West Africans who survived a slave shipwreck and settled on the Island of St. Vincent. Despite being forcefully uprooted from their ancestral homeland—torn from their roots, families, and cultural traditions—the Garifuna people demonstrated extraordinary perseverance. When ultimately expelled from their island home, they arrived on Belize's shores in humble raft boats, carrying with them a legacy of resilience. Families began to build independent lives outside the logging camps, settling in small villages and creating a culture that blended African roots with the realities of colonial society. The abolition of slavery created space for new cultural expressions and community building. Against the odds, they have managed to preserve their distinctive Garifuna language through generations, carrying it forward as a living testament to their identity and spirit. Today, the Garifuna proudly converse in their native tongue among themselves, and their commitment to cultural survival is evident in their determination to teach the Garifuna language to their children.

During my initial research into the Creole community of Belize, I was struck by an intriguing detail: in Belize, the word "Creole" is most often spelled "Kriol." This was different from the spelling I was accustomed to in the standard English lexicon, and it piqued my curiosity about language and cultural adaptation in this small Central American nation. With its modern Creole culture, Belize is the only English-speaking country in Central America. Belize's colonial history sets it apart. Independence from Britain came only in 1981, at which time the sense of new beginnings was palpable. Emancipation in Belize marked both a turning point and the start of new struggles. Today, Emancipation Day is observed on August 1st and is not only as a commemoration of freedom but also as a reminder of the long road toward progress that continues to shape Belizean culture and linguistics.

The more I learned about the Garifuna—their cultural traditions, including the colorful traditional dresses complete with head wraps of the Garifuna women and the styles and patterns of the Garifuna men's clothing, the varieties of the Garifuna ethnic foods, their music, and dances—the more they reminded me of the people of Sierra Leone. I felt a growing sense of kinship. The faces in the pictures sometimes resembled my own. Their foods, their customs, their very spirit called to me, as if I were hearing a familiar song in a new language. I needed to explore this burgeoning connection I felt.

After much learning and reflection, I became convinced that Belize could be my next home, even though it was thousands of miles away from the village where I was born. The two countries—Sierra Leone and Belize—felt connected in my heart and mind. Belize's proximity to the United States was convenient, and the fact that English is the official language made the idea of communication less daunting. All these factors made the idea of relocating more and more appealing, especially since I would be among people with similar cultural and traditional backgrounds.

The legacy of emancipation is not just a matter of history—it is alive in the rhythms of everyday Belizean life. I wanted to experience for myself how this hard-fought freedom has shaped the people, the culture, and the land. But before making such a life-altering decision, I knew I had to see Belize for myself. So, on the 19th of December, 2016, I boarded a flight from St. Louis, Missouri, to Belize City. Once I landed at around 12:00 in the afternoon, I made a beeline for the home of the Garifuna. I took the James Bus Line to Punta Gorda, a lush town at the southernmost tip of the country. Punta Gorda isn't the most popular destination for tourists; it is yet peaceful and beautiful. The James Bus Line features converted school buses that traverse the countryside taking people from Belize City to villages and towns in the South. The bus seats were cramped, and the tour bus traversed the country roads slowly. The bus has no room for long legs like mine. My legs ached after being cramped between the seats. The Belizean bus driver told me that most people consider Punta Gorda a dead-end town because there is only one way in and one way out of the town, and it does not cater to tourists like other towns around the country. Along the ride I saw the tropical green forest of Belmopan and the high Maya mountains. We stopped at various bus stations for 15-minute breaks. I appreciated the opportunity to stretch my legs and use the rest room. The bus ride from Belize City to Punta Gorda took eight hours—seven hours of anticipation and wonder.

I walked into the St. Charles Inn around 7:30 at night. I'd made my reservation for the Inn prior to leaving the United States. The bell attached to the front door chimed as I walked in, and I took in the scenery of the Inn's lobby. It was modest, but to me everything was exotic and wrapped in magic.

I was greeted by Mr. Charles Wagner, a spritely, short, bald man in his 80s, who walked with a cane. Mr. Wagner greeted me by name. "You must be Mr. Mandewah? We've been expecting you. How was your trip?" I was filled with glee by the first hint of belonging.

I settled into my room, and almost immediately I felt hunger pangs. I tucked my wallet on a chain into my shirt and headed back down to the lobby. Mr. Wagner was nowhere to be found. I wandered out into the street and began to walk the Boulevard. I found a small restaurant just two doors down from the Inn that was still open. I sat down for a meal of rice and beans and fried plantain. I felt invigorated. I hadn't eaten all day.

After a restful night's sleep, I woke up early to begin my exploration. I had ten days to vet the town. On day two, I met Keisha Zuniga. I was walking along the street and saw a row of shops. I walked up to a small salon and saw a woman braiding hair. I was fascinated. The woman who was doing the braiding noticed me watching through the window and gestured for me to enter.

"Hello," Keisha said with the enthusiasm of a tour guide. I greeted her in return. She acknowledged my accent and asked, "Are you visiting here?"

I gave her what would become my repeated refrain: "My name is Francis Mandewah. I am originally from Sierra Leone, but I am also an American citizen. I am in Punta Gorda searching for my retirement home."

She smiled broadly, and I knew we would be friends. Keisha is a Garifuna secondary school teacher with a degree in English from the University of Belize. Her deep knowledge of Garifuna history, not just in Belize but also in Honduras, Guatemala, and Nicaragua, was invaluable. I soaked up every story like a sponge. She invited me to meet her family.

Through our many conversations over the next week, I shared my growing affection for Punta Gorda, its warm-hearted people, the tropical beauty of the land, and my special admiration for the Garifuna community. I arrived at the conclusion that I would, in fact, relocate, settle, and retire in this Caribbean haven; it became crystal clear: Punta Gorda, Belize, would be my new home away from Sierra Leone and the United States.

As a person who has a deep interest in culture, I made it a personal mission to seek out the pillars of Belize's Creole community. One legendary name stood out: Ms. Leela Vernon, an iconic figure in Belize's cultural and musical landscape, celebrated countrywide as a living embodiment of Creole drama, music, and history.

I had read extensively about Ms. Vernon, who was often cited as the "Queen of Brok Don," a pioneering force whose choreography, musical composition, and commanding performances had taken Creole culture to stages across the globe. During my visit to Punta Gorda, I was thrilled to discover that Ms. Vernon lived on Front Street, her home facing the ever-changing blues of the Caribbean Sea.

Eager with anticipation, I approached the modest compound shaded by tropical trees. As I walked through the gate, a short, friendly gentleman sporting dreadlocks approached and greeted me with an infectious warmth.

"Is Ms. Leela Vernon home?" I asked.

He smiled, "Yes, I am one of her sons. My name is Francz Vernon." With genuine hospitality, he led me through the house to a cozy living room where Ms. Vernon herself reclined in a gently rocking chair.

Leela Vernon

21 Oct 1950 - 19 Feb 2017

I introduced myself with earnest respect, singing my frequent refrain, "Well, hello, Ms. Vernon, my name is Francis Mandewah. I am originally from Sierra Leone but am now an American citizen, and I'm visiting Punta Gorda for the first time with the plans of retiring here."

Ms. Vernon immediately extended both of her hands toward me with dignified grace. Stepping forward to accept her greeting, I took both her hands in mine as a greeting. Her skin was smooth. She held my hands firmly for just a moment then released her grip and let her fingertips slide over the length of my hands. She kept her brown eyes fixed on mine.

Before I even had a chance to sit, Ms. Vernon asked, "Are you from Freetown the capital city of Sierra Leone?"

When I confirmed that I was from a village just outside of Freetown, her face broke into a radiant smile as she clapped her hands together then cupped her face with her hands.

"Welcome, welcome! Freetown, Sierra Leone is very important to us Creoles here in Belize because there is a direct connection between the Creoles of Belize and the Creoles in Freetown, Sierra Leone."

Her words echoed deep layers of shared history, spanning continents and centuries. She continued, "In fact, one of the major streets in Belize City is named Freetown Road, so you are welcome among your people here in Belize and here in Punta Gorda."

As we conversed, Francz Vernon offered me a cup brimming with fresh, sweet coconut water. I accepted it gratefully, savoring the refreshing taste while expressing how honored I was to be in Ms. Vernon's presence—a feeling that brought me emotionally closer to my ancestral Creole heritage in Sierra Leone.

Ms. Vernon smiled and said, "We are pleased to receive and have you here in Belize." I thanked her for such heartfelt hospitality, feeling an immediate sense of acceptance. I took a few moments to share with her my journey, touching on the path that led me from Sierra Leone to America—where I studied, worked, and eventually retired—and then to Belize, a country I hoped to make my sanctuary in my later years. Listening intently, Ms. Vernon repeated her warm welcome and began recounting her own experiences aiding Africans who arrived in Punta Gorda.

"I took lots of Africans into my home who came off the boat right here in front of my home. Many were "illegals" and didn't have visas to come to

Belize. I took them in every other week, fed them, gave them a place to sleep until they were ready to continue their journeys to the north and to the United States."

As Ms. Vernon spoke, her voice filled with empathy and resolve, my memory flashed to my own arduous journey—being smuggled into Algeria after a perilous crossing of the Sahara Desert in an open-air convoy, all in pursuit of a new life in America.

Even as she recounted her generous acts of kindness, my curiosity was burning to hear more about her remarkable contributions to Belizean music and culture. Seizing a pause in her story, I asked—brimming with admiration— about her impact and her storied career. Ms. Vernon straightened with pride and replied, "Well, my brother, I wrote and choreographed the national music of Belize that is called 'Brok Don.' I was given the official title by the government of Belize as the Queen of Brok Don. I have performed in London for Queen Elizabeth II. I also performed for Queen Elizabeth II right here in Punta Gorda when she came to Belize to hand us our Independence. I have performed in the United States, in Mexico, and across South America. And I have taught lots of Belizeans. I had a whole band with different musicians and different instruments. I mostly sang and danced to the Brok Don tunes and rhythms. So, I have made my own impact on Belize. Now, I am at home, retired, and enjoying seeing my grandchildren grow."

I couldn't help but ask if I could buy one of her CDs. She waved the idea away with a gentle protest, "You don't have to pay me for it. Here is one for you for free." Accepting her gift with gratitude, I bade her farewell, expressing how much I looked forward to seeing her again once I was settled into Punta Gorda.

As I was making my return trip to St. Louis, Missouri, to complete my final preparations before embarking on my drive south to Belize. I took a purposeful detour and stopped in Belize City. My destination was the office of the National Kriol Council. By good fortune, both the President and Vice President happened to be in the office that day.

Upon entering the building, I was greeted by a tall, slender, dark-skinned woman, radiating both dignity and warmth. She extended her hand and introduced herself as Myrna Manzanares, president of the National Kriol Council of Belize—a renowned educator and champion of Kriol heritage.

Just a moment later, her deputy, a poised and engaging woman, stepped out from her office and shook my hand warmly. "My name is Dana Rhamdas. What can we help you with today?"

I introduced myself, singing my common refrain, "My name is Francis Mandewah. I am originally from Sierra Leone..." As soon as the words left my lips, both Myrna and Dana exchanged a knowing glance and, almost in unison, responded with, "Freetown, Sierra Leone?"

Myrna Manzanares
30 Oct 1946 – 21 Dec 2021

Their immediate recognition of my homeland filled me with an unexpected sense of connection and kinship, and underscored the historic ties—woven through centuries of the shared experiences of diaspora all over the world.

I continued, "I'm also an American citizen, and I've chosen to retire in Belize, down in Punta Gorda." Both women smiled broadly, expressing their delight that I had made the journey and sought out their office to build a bridge between our communities.

Myrna took a seat beside me and launched into a passionate and illuminating explanation of the Council's work.

"One of our main roles," she said, "is to ensure that the rich history and enduring legacy of the Kriol community in Belize continues to flourish."

She paused for emphasis, then stood up and went into her office, returning moments later with a large, sturdy volume in her arms.

She placed it on the desk in front of me with gentle pride and said, "This is the *Belize Kriol Dictionary*. I collaborated closely with the Government of Belize and the Ministry of Culture, working nearly four years to bring this to life. Every word and every definition in the book is rooted in the everyday Kriol spoken in Belize. Our aim is to maintain the continuity and vibrancy of our language for generations to come."

She continued, "Kriol isn't unique to Belize. It's spoken in many places around the world—in Nova Scotia, Canada, in the bayous of Louisiana, and elsewhere. Each region has its own flavor, its own variations in pronunciation and vocabulary. But this dictionary is specifically anchored in the language of our Belizean people."

I was genuinely impressed by the scholarly dedication and scope of her work. Each page featured the English and Kriol definitions, along with phonetic spellings/pronunciations of each word. I commended her for such a significant academic and cultural contribution.

"How can I get one of your dictionaries?" I asked. To my delight, she told me I could buy one for $20.00 BZD, and I gratefully made the purchase right then.

Though I was eager to ask Ms. Manzanares why the Creole of Belize had adopted the spelling "Kriol," I decided to save my question for another day—perhaps after I'd settled into my new home, soaked up more of the local culture, and had a chance to study the dictionary. Flipping through the thick pages of my new Kriol Dictionary, I marveled at the linguistic richness captured on every page.

During our conversation, Dana Rhamdas turned to me with curiosity about my background. "Tell me about the Creole spoken in Sierra Leone. Are you a Creole from Freetown, the city where most of the Sierra Leonean Creole community is found?"

I responded, "Actually, I'm not from Freetown, nor am I part of the Creole community. I was born in the eastern part of Sierra Leone, roughly 200 miles from Freetown, and I'm from the Mende tribe. Sierra Leone is a tapestry of diversity, home to twelve major tribes and as many distinct languages—but Creole is the lingua franca; it's the language that everyone across the country understands and speaks to communicate."

With a welcoming smile, Ms. Myrna encouraged me, "When you finally move to Belize, keep in touch with the Kriol Council. We'd be happy to help you as you settle in and learn more about the Kriol culture here."

The time I spent with them flew by. I had to say my goodbyes and head to the airport. I placed my precious Kriol Dictionary securely in my suitcase and hurried to catch my flight back to St. Louis. I carried with me not only a new book but a new sense of belonging and anticipation. I was about to embark on a journey that would bridge continents—not just in geography, but in language, culture, and the enduring bonds of human connection. It added extra anticipation and excitement about my upcoming migration to Belize.

~~~~

I returned to St. Louis and began preparing for my big move. I researched the costs of shipping my belongings then flying to Belize, but I found it cost prohibitive. Ultimately, I chose a more adventurous route: driving my 2003 Hyundai Elantra GT, a clunker of a car I'd bought from a Milwaukee salvage yard in 2009, all the way to Belize. I'd only be able to take what I could carry. The thought of driving an old vehicle through Mexico stirred memories of another perilous journey—my crossing of the Sahara Desert 43 years prior. That experience, still vivid in my mind, reminded me of the time I was left to die in the sand, only to be rescued by a compassionate Tuareg man and his wife, who nursed me back to life. The memory brought a shiver of unease, but also a surge of determination. I had faced death before and survived by the grace of God, my own resilience, and the kindness of strangers. This new journey would be another test of my resolve.

I knew the risks of driving through Mexico, where stories of gangs, drug dealers, and highway bandits are all too common. Determined to be prudent, I resolved to drive only during daylight hours—a well-known precaution among seasoned American and Canadian travelers. I traced the path on the map and watched news alerts.

I thoroughly researched all the requirements for vehicle insurance and registration to drive through Mexico. Online, I purchased the auto insurance policy required to drive through Mexico. I made multiple copies of the Mexican auto insurance policy and my State of Missouri vehicle registration along with copies of my driver's license to keep separate from the original documents as advised. The website said the copies were for showing Mexican immigration, police, and at the checkpoints inside of Mexico.

The overland journey from St. Louis to Punta Gorda would span 2,450 miles, so I took every possible precaution to ensure my car was up to the task. I took the car to a trusted mechanic in Ferguson, MO for a complete diagnostic. Old and potentially faulty parts were replaced, at considerable expense, but I knew it was a necessary investment.

When the mechanic asked why I was replacing still-functioning parts, I hesitated to reveal my true destination. I didn't want anyone to dissuade me from this adventure. I simply replied, "It's always a good idea to take preventative care on old vehicles."

His response about my Hyundai's engine reassured me. "This 2.0 engine is the best Hyundai ever built. The entire engine and its parts are all built from aluminum, not steel, so you can drive it forever if you take care of it. My daughter had the same model, and it never let her down." His words pushed me on, fueling my hope that my car would carry me safely to Belize.

I consider myself an action-oriented person. I rationally analyze the pros and cons of a situation, and I calculate the associated risks. Life's adventures always involve risks. And in my opinion, this adventure was well worth taking for the benefits of experience and knowledge to be gained in the process.

The mechanic's confidence and my own determination not withstanding, doubts lingered. Despite all of my fears and anticipations, I'm a firm believer that God always works through people, and that God always uses people as instruments of His peace. I was fortunate in the Sahara Desert to be rescued by a good Samaritan, but there was no guarantee whether or not God would again rescue me should I have mechanical issues or encounter problems with Mexican bandits, gang members, or drug dealers along the way. All I could do was hope for divine intervention should the need arise.

I buttressed myself with assurances from my faith. Just as it was faith and determination that gave me the power to endure all the challenges in crossing the Sahara Desert, I knew I had to continue to rely on God and my faith, along with my measured determination, to drive through Mexico without incident and safely arrive in Punta Gorda, Belize.

Preparation to relocate to a tropical country steeped in temperatures above an almost unwavering eighty-nine degrees year-round meant a serious wardrobe overhaul. I donated all my winter clothes to Goodwill, Salvation Army, and St. Vincent de Paul. I scoured those same stores repeatedly, searching for lightweight shirts, shorts, and sandals. Despite the stigma some attach to used clothing, I was amazed by the quality and abundance of nearly-new, brand-name items, especially at St. Vincent de Paul. Most donations came from affluent people, and the clothes and furniture were almost as good as new.

While I was packing, I went through a morass of papers and documents to determine which were still relevant and which were outdated or irrelevant and needed to be discarded. Sorting through my possessions, I faced the hardest task of all: deciding which books to keep. Over the years, I have amassed books from prominent and classical authors that I dearly admire. Books that continue to have an impact on me and on my perspective and outlook on life and on humanity. I am not particularly materialistic; however, I felt a strong attachment to my books. I had donated clothes, what-nots, furniture, and more, but my books were the hardest things for me to let go of.

Certain books really speak to me, particularly the ones where I can relate to the themes the authors depict. Thomas More's fictitious *Utopia* juxtaposed with the false dreams of colonialism; the stories told in *The Classic Slum* by Robert Roberts; *Same Kind of Different as Me* by Ron Hall and Denver Moore reminds me of my friendship with Tom Johnson, a white man from a different background who met me and voluntarily chose to give me support that transformed my life from desperation in Sierra Leone to freedom and opportunity in America, much like the white man, Ron Hall lifted up the black homeless man, Denver Moore; *Religions of the World* by Gerald L. Berry; and *Things Fall Apart* by Chinua Achebe; and the powerful survival tools laid out in *Live and Be Free Through Psycho-Cybernetics* by Maxwell Maltz, M.D., F.I.C.S. Books are heavy and hard to transport, but they are like old friends—

impossible to leave behind. I kept a few and let go of the rest, certain that I would be blessed to accumulate a new collection in my new home.

~~~~

After servicing my car and buying a new wardrobe, I looked at my bank balance and realized I needed to preserve every penny to successfully transition from the United States to Belize. My savings were meager, and I intended to gather everything that was owed to me. My attention turned to the security deposit on my apartment.

Too many landlords in Saint Louis are notorious for, and skillful at, avoiding refunding a tenant's security deposit. I did everything in my power to avoid giving my landlord an excuse for not refunding my $1,200 security deposit. I carefully reread my rental contract and agreement. Since there was no damage to the apartment during my occupancy, I turned my attention to the clause on cleaning fees. I did everything I could to the inside of my apartment to make it appear exactly as it was when I initially moved in.

My work friend, Fred, volunteered to come over and walk through prior to the landlord coming over. I scrubbed the toilet bowl and shower spotless, I used bleach and Pine-Sol for the kitchen counters.

"Are you going to polish the floors?" Fred asked.

"They weren't shined when I moved in," I retorted.

"Better safe than sorry. Don't give them an in."

I went out and bought wood polish and polished the floors. I left the refrigerator and the stove spotless. I cleaned the inside of the cabinets and underneath the kitchen sink to perfection. I spent hours before vacating my apartment, ensuring everything was right. I was determined to get my full security deposit back.

I continued to be concerned that the landlord would find anything he could to prevent my receipt of a full refund, but I was determined to win at this game. At the final inspection of the apartment, the landlord brought a very bright, high voltage torch light which he used to scrutinize every corner— underneath the cabinets, the kitchen counters, all over the bathroom, he even flashed the bright light up on the ceiling.

After he had thoroughly inspected the two bedrooms, he turned to me and paused. He held his breath for a moment and finally said, "Make sure the office has your forwarding address where we can send your full deposit refund."

Sweet success! I felt a wave of relief—he could have found any excuse to keep my money, but I outsmarted him with my attention to detail, having had the discipline to clean things right. On the broad scheme of things it was a small victory, but I took it as a sign that my approach to this process was going to result in success. There was no need to fear.

As my departure drew near, I debated whether to tell my African friends and relatives about my solo drive through Mexico. In the end, I kept my plans to myself. I didn't want anyone to plant seeds of fear or try to talk me out of it by attempting to dissuade me from driving to Belize.

My life has always been about facing challenges and taking risks—some regrettable, but many I managed to survive and some I even triumphed over.

Unlike me, none of my friends or relatives had crossed the Sahara or sailed the high seas to reach America; their journeys were easier, less fraught with danger. They had never experienced or had to face trials and tribulations like I had experienced and endured. Thus, they would not have any context for understanding my choices.

~~~~

I couldn't leave without saying goodbye to someone dear to me from my religious community. So, days before I would put my foot to the pedal and leave on my journey, I visited Sister Rosanne in South St. Louis one last time. She was just leaving the chapel when I entered the Provincial Home. We convened in the guest room. I felt happy in the presence of this pious woman who has known me since I was 14 years old, way back in 1976 when I was a student at Yengema Secondary School in Sierra Leone. I stayed in contact with her since 1976 to present, and I was grateful to her for writing the foreword to my book: *Friendship: A True Story of Adventure, Goodwill, and Endurance* that I published in March of 2016. I chose her to write the foreword because she knew the spiritual side of my journey. She had prayed with me and for me since I was a boy, and I could not think of a better person to speak for me.

Before I could utter a word, Sister Rosanne asked how my book was doing, and before I could even say a word, the 79-year-old Catholic nun continued, saying to me, "Francis, it is a good book. I was more than happy to write the foreword. Your book has the potential to make an impact in the lives of other people, but don't expect to get rich from it."

"I recognize the truth in your words, Sister. I did not do it for the money. I've accomplished my goal though, and what's more I'm happy to report that my book has been adapted to a screenplay because of the inspiring nature of my story. I have dreams of it being in the theaters one day."

She gave a knowing nod. "As long as you acknowledge that success is not always measured in monetary terms."

Over the years of our relationship, Sister Rosanne imparted straight talk, disciplinary advice, and counsel.

I responded to Sister Rosanne by saying, "I am grateful that I have written a book that honors the life and legacy of Captain Thomas Johnson, who was the American pilot from Minnesota that was employed in the diamond mines in my hometown region. I am eternally grateful that Tom gave me generous support to get an education, brought me to the United States and paid all of my college expenses so I could realize my American dream. It was truly an act of goodwill and generosity that transformed my life."

Sister Rosanne responded, "Well, I am gratified that the main purpose of your book has been achieved. I am glad that you are grateful for what God has done in your life. This is the right attitude."

With a smile on my face, I looked at her and unveiled the reason for my visit: to give her my big news, saying, "Sister, I have come to say goodbye. I am leaving for Belize, Central America in three days. I have decided to spend my retirement years living in Belize."

Sister Rosanne took a pause and looked me straight in the eyes and said, "Well, Francis, I have known you since you were only 14 years old. You have overcome so many challenges in your life… You are no stranger to hardship and overcoming difficulties. But the important thing is you have never stopped persevering. If you really set your mind to something, I see you succeed every time. That makes you more likely to succeed again, because you just don't give up. I believe in you." Then she added, "Tell me, do you know anyone in Belize?" and followed up with the question I wished she hadn't asked: how long is the flight to Belize?"

I stretched my neck anxiously and murmured quietly, "Sister, I am driving to Belize." I was afraid that she would try to dissuade me, but instead, she just gave me practical and spiritual advice. She said, "Well, make sure your vehicle is safe and completely maintained. And keep praying. I will keep you in my prayers." I was relieved to receive her supportive reply in the face of the challenge I was taking on. I hadn't realized the value of validation before she offered it to me. I stood up as she was about to leave. I hugged her and said goodbye. I walked to the lobby, signed out of the Visitor Log and exited the Provincial Home, on the path to my new life.

As I steered my car toward the hotel where I was staying just days before my departure, my mind buzzed with indecision. Should I tell Rev. Fr. Rose Roseborough—the beloved priest at Blessed Teresa Calcutta parish in Ferguson, my current spiritual home—that I was about to leave the United States behind and embark on a bold drive to Belize? The thought weighed on me as I navigated the familiar streets of St. Louis, the gravity of my impending journey settling in.

The morning after my visit with Sister Rosanne I went to my church. Sunlight filtered through stained glass during Sunday Mass. The church was filled with the comforting murmur of prayers and the scent of incense. After the service, I made it a point to shake Fr. Rose's hand, feeling warmth and kindness in his grip. Yet, I kept my secret close to my chest, choosing not to share my plans with him or any of my fellow parishioners. Privacy felt essential; this was a farewell I needed to keep to myself. No need for fanfare, just a quiet exit. I had been a wallflower and a wallflower I would remain. I savored my final moments with the parish community, quietly slipping out into the world beyond the church doors, my heart both heavy and hopeful.

After Mass, I made a quick stop at the gas station. The hiss of the pump and the rich aroma of gasoline filled the air as I topped off my tank with Shell V-Power, the highest grade fuel I could find. My Hyundai Elantra GT would need every ounce of power for the long road ahead, stretching all the way south to Belize. I stood at the pump fantasizing about my journey and my future in Punta Gorda.

Chapter 2

THE SKY WAS still dark when I pulled onto Highway 70 East out of Ferguson, Missouri, my 2003 Hyundai Elantra GT packed to the brim with only the bare essentials for life in Belize's subtropical climate. The early hours of April 27, 2017, felt electric with possibility. As I merged onto Interstate 55, heading toward Memphis, Tennessee, the City of St. Louis faded in my rearview mirror. To my left, the mighty Mississippi River shimmered under the morning light; to my right, the city's skyline stood tall and silent. I waved a quiet goodbye to St. Louis, feeling a bittersweet mix of nostalgia and excitement. So many memories—some cherished, some challenging—floated through my mind as I crossed that threshold.

The drive began smoothly, my car responding eagerly despite its heavy load. I stuck to the right lane, content to move at my own pace, grateful for the wide multi-lane American highways. Compared to the narrow, winding roads I'd seen from the passenger seat in Europe, the Interstate felt vast and forgiving. I felt a new appreciation for the luxury of space American highways provided.

I kept my speed around 50 miles per hour, letting the faster cars zip past me. Occasionally, impatient drivers honked or glared as they overtook my slow-moving vehicle. A few State highway patrol cars passed by, but none bothered me, perhaps understanding that a heavily loaded car on a long journey has its own rhythm. I reminded myself not to let the frustrations of others disturb my peace; people will feel what they feel, regardless of my agenda.

As the miles rolled by, I felt a sense of relief knowing my auto insurance and AAA policy were still valid as I crossed into Tennessee, then Arkansas, Louisiana, and Texas. The safety net of roadside assistance was a comfort, a small shield against the unknown. But I knew that once I crossed into Mexico, that safety net would vanish. Based on my research and the messages from American and Canadian expats on Facebook it was clear: driving through Mexico at night was dangerous, and roadside help was nonexistent. For now, though, I was cocooned in the conveniences of the American highway system through to the Texas-Mexico border in Brownsville, Texas, hoping that luck and preparation would see me safely through the challenges ahead.

The journey south was thankfully uneventful. I was grateful that the highways were clear and there was no major construction. Despite the horns and impatient glances from fellow travelers, I kept both hands on the steering wheel, focused on my own journey, determined not to let their irritation become my burden. The road stretched endlessly ahead, a ribbon of possibility leading me toward a new life.

After about five hours of driving, I saw the signs for Memphis and before long, I was crossing a bridge over the legendary Mississippi River—the same river I had bid farewell to in St. Louis just hours earlier. The Mississippi, America's longest river, winds its way through the heart of the country, connecting States and stories. As I gazed at its powerful current, I marveled at the sheer scale and significance of the waterway.

As I proceeded over the bridge, memories flooded back to my time as a probation and parole agent in Hayward, Wisconsin, I crossed the Mississippi many times, traveling to Minneapolis and St. Cloud, Minnesota, to visit my friend Tom Johnson's mother, Virginia, in Milaca. Later, when I worked as an Education Counselor at the State of Illinois Department of Corrections in East St. Louis, I crossed the river every morning, moving between States.

Now, as I continued toward the State of Mississippi, the river remained on my mind. I wondered if I would cross it one final time in Louisiana before leaving the United States for good, my sights set on Belize and the unknown adventures that awaited me beyond the border. With every mile, the anticipation grew. I was leaving behind the familiar, propelled by a mix of nerves and exhilaration, ready to embrace whatever the road—and fate—had in store.

I have traveled and lived in many different States across America, but curiously, I had never set foot in Mississippi. Despite this, I was deeply aware of the State's pivotal role in the American social landscape—a battleground where history was shaped by courage and sacrifice. As I crossed the border and saw the bold sign welcoming me to the "State of Mississippi," right beside the familiar golden arches of a McDonald's. At the exit for the city of Jackson, I felt compelled to pause my journey. It was the perfect moment to take a break, grab a Big Mac, and reflect on the monumental significance of this place. How appropriate for me to explore my country once more before leaving.

As I steered my car along the sun-drenched streets, my mind wandered to a different kind of journey—a journey marked by the hard-won victories of the civil rights movement. Their victories gave me the power to fight for my rights and ultimately keep my job at the Wisconsin Department of Corrections until retirement. I attribute my victory in federal court to the civil rights struggles of the men and women in the State of Mississippi. I am filled with gratitude for their courage against insurmountable odds.

Inside the bustling McDonald's in Jackson, I took a seat and unwrapped my Big Mac, savoring the first few hearty bites and washing them down with an ice-cold Coke. As I sat there, I found myself lost in thought, honoring the countless individuals who had fought—and in many cases, given their lives—for the American way of life right there in Jackson. Their bravery and sacrifices were not just stories from the past; they were the very reason I could enjoy this simple lunch, sitting among people of all backgrounds. The realization struck me with force: without struggles and victories, my own life would have been drastically different. I thanked them and humbled myself to them for their struggles and sacrifice.

My mind drifted to Tom Johnson, the man who made my American journey possible. Tom was a pilot and decorated Vietnam War hero from Milaca, Minnesota, working in the diamond mines of Sierra Leone when our paths crossed. If not for his extraordinary kindness, I would never have left my village, went to Europe, come to America, attended college, or applied for State job. I owe every achievement in my American life to Tom's generosity—a white man from a different world, who saw something in me and chose to help.

I've never forgotten Tom Johnson's words of wisdom, advice and encouragement he said to me at my graduation ceremony in Springfield, Massachusetts. When a newspaper reporter with a yellow notepad and a pen in her hand asked Tom about his relationship with me, Tom responded saying,

"It's a long story, but suffice it to say, as Christians when we see a need it is our duty to help to make a difference in someone's life. I met Francis in Sierra Leone, and I saw a need and have done my part… Thank you. I've got a plane to catch."

Tom was aware that in spite of my academic achievements, as a person of color, I would encounter challenges in my job search and possibly at my place of employment. Thus, his exact words of wisdom and encouragement to me were: "Francis, America is not a perfect country, but there are opportunities here. Keep hope alive, you have come a long way. God always works through people."

I looked up at him and I responded while nodding my head and saying, "Yes, Tom, you are completely correct. God always works through people." I nodded, feeling the truth of his words.

"Yes, Tom, you are completely correct. God always works through people. It was God who worked through you the day you met me selling oranges at the National Diamond Mining Company (NDMC) headquarters at Yengema and befriended me. It was God who worked through you to bring me to America, led you to pay my tuition, and provide my room and board, so I could realize the American dream."

Tom smiled and replied, "You got the point. God always works through people, Francis."

That lunch in the Jackson McDonald's became a humbling and sacred moment. As I left, I paused in the parking lot to gaze at the impressive State Capitol building, letting the weight of history and gratitude settle over me. Then, I climbed back into my car and merged onto the highway 65 south, heading toward Louisiana, my mind alive with reflection.

As I drove I remember how difficult it was to attain my first State position. Despite holding a Master's degree in Public Administration—a credential that far exceeded the Associate's and Bachelor's degrees of other applicants—I found myself repeatedly overlooked for a position I was more than qualified to fill. Three times I sat through interviews, three times I emerged as the most qualified candidate, yet I was passed over. Each rejection letter from human resources stung, but they always included a line encouraging me to reapply. It was as if hope itself was being rationed out in small, cautious doses.

Still, I refused to let disappointment extinguish my hope. On my third attempt, I submitted my application and braced myself for another round of waiting. Every morning, I peered anxiously through my window, searching for the familiar silhouette of the mailman, my heart leaping with every envelope that landed in my mailbox. Weeks slipped by with no word. The silence grew heavier with each passing day, threatening to smother the last embers of my optimism.

Then, one morning as I was preparing eggs and toast for breakfast, the shrill ring of the phone shattered the quiet. I snatched it up. "Hello, this is Francis Mandewah," I said, my voice trembling just a little.

On the other end, a calm, professional voice replied, "Hello, is this Mr. Francis Mandewah?" I confirmed, and she introduced herself. "My name is Kathleen Lelinski. I'm the Regional Secretary for the Department of Corrections in the Milwaukee Office. I'm calling to let you know that you have been selected and offered the position of probation and parole officer."

The words echoed in my ears, almost too good to be true. Before I could even respond, Ms. Lelinski continued, "I need the names and telephone numbers of two character references who are not related to you. Please call me within three days with that information. Congratulations, and good luck."

With that, she hung up, leaving me standing in the kitchen, phone in hand, overwhelmed with gratitude and disbelief.

I dropped to my knees right there on the kitchen floor and thanked God with all my heart. But mere gratitude didn't seem enough—I clenched my fists, leapt into the air, and let out a shout of pure joy, nearly hitting my head on the ceiling. The triumph was electric, coursing through my veins.

That evening, my girlfriend Wanda came over after work and immediately noticed the radiant smile lighting up my face—a smile she hadn't seen in a long time. She studied me for a long moment, her eyes narrowing with suspicion and anticipation.

"Did you get the State job?" She finally asked. I nodded vigorously, unable to contain my excitement.

"Yes!" I exclaimed. She rushed into my arms, hugging me with a passion and relief that spoke volumes.

Months later, as I settled into my new role, I had an unexpected encounter that shed light on the forces that had shaped my journey. My immediate supervisor, an African American woman, stopped by my office to discuss a case.

As our meeting ended and she prepared to leave, she paused at the door, turned back and said, "You need to thank Kathleen Lelinski. She stood up for you."

With that, she was gone, leaving me alone with my thoughts.

I leaned back in my chair, gazing up at the ceiling, and remembered the words of my friend and mentor, Tom Johnson: "God always works through people."

I offered another prayer of thanks, this time specifically for Kathleen Lelinski.

Before that phone call I had no idea who Kathleen Lelinski was. She was a complete stranger—someone from a different background, a different world. And yet, in a crucial moment, she had chosen to stand up for me. I imagined the scene behind closed doors during the final selection process. I pictured her speaking up, perhaps saying, "Look, this candidate, Francis Mandewah, holds a master's degree in public administration. None of our previous hires have a master's degree. He's more qualified than anyone we've brought on board so far. He's been interviewed three times. We can't keep overlooking him. I vote that we hire Mr. Mandewah."

The fact that Kathleen Lelinski, a white woman, would advocate for me so passionately reminded me that goodness and integrity know no boundaries of race, culture, or background. Her courage and fairness changed the trajectory of my life. Without her intervention, I might have been passed over yet again, and the State of Wisconsin might have continued to hire less qualified candidates.

I only ever got the opportunity to meet Kathleen once. Our paths crossed at the copy machine one day. She walked up to me and introduced herself and quickly walked away before I could say anything—to thank her.

Reflecting on it all, I am convinced that it was God's hand guiding Kathleen Lelinski to become an instrument of peace and justice, transforming not only my life but the lives of others who would follow. I will always remember Tom Johnson's wisdom: God works through people. And in my case, he worked through a stranger named Kathleen Lelinski, a woman whose quiet bravery made all the difference.

Chapter 3

FOR A BRIEF moment as I cruised toward the State of Louisiana, my thoughts drifted away from the road ahead. Instead, I found myself lost in memories of my past struggles living and working in Wisconsin. The anticipation of what lay before me mingled with reflections on the journey I'd already taken, filling the car with a sense of both pain about the past and hope for the future. I'd spent 15 years living and working in an environment where very few people looked like me, and now I was going to reside in a human tapestry, filled with people of all nationalities, colors, and religions.

That first night in Louisiana, I found myself in a small, charming town called Amity. The air was thick with southern humidity, and the neon lights of the local motel flickered as I settled in for some much-needed rest. The next morning, with the sun barely peeking over the horizon, I got to work preparing for another long day on the road. I popped the hood of my Hyundai Elantra GT and carefully checked every fluid level—oil, coolant, brake fluid—making sure everything was just right. I inspected the pressure on my brand-new Firestone tires, feeling a surge of confidence in my trusty vehicle. Taking these simple measures gave me confidence. If there was to be an issue, it wouldn't be from these basic things. Satisfied that everything was in order, I pulled out of the parking lot, merged into the steady flow of traffic, and set my sights on the buzzing energy of Houston, Texas.

The drive through Louisiana was at first, uneventful. The roads were smooth, and the scenery was lush with green fields and towering cypress trees draped in Spanish moss that hung like wet lace in the soggy southern air. But then, out of nowhere, I approached the Dat Lake Charles bridge which is so steep it looks like it belongs in a movie—rising up before me like the very summit of the Great Pyramid of Egypt. As I merged into the slow-moving traffic inching its way up the incline, the pace slowed to a crawl and then suddenly, to a complete stop. I found myself sandwiched between two vehicles stranded in the middle of the bridge, with nowhere to go.

As I sat there, foot pressed firmly on the brake, a wave of anxiety washed over me. Thoughts began to crawl through my mind. What if my engine overheated? Even though I had just installed a brand-new radiator, the scenarios gnawed at me. I tried to reassure myself, recalling the mechanic's words about my Elantra GT—how it was built to "never die," equipped with one of the best engines Hyundai ever built. Still, the fear lingered as we crept slowly toward the bridge's pinnacle. I felt every vibration. Everything I saw and heard had a hidden meaning.

Finally, we reached the top and the descent began. It felt almost like a rollercoaster with cars nose-diving down the steep slope in a slow, cautious procession. My mind raced with another worry: What if my brakes failed? I replaced the calipers, brake shoes, and pads, but the thought of rear-ending the car in front of me was hard to shake. I remembered other nerve-wrecking bridges I'd crossed—the Chesapeake Bay Bridge, that stretched for four miles over open water between Maryland and Delaware. Like I did so many times on my daily commute, I prayed. I asked that His mercy cover me as I drove. Through it all, my car performed flawlessly, carrying me ever closer to Texas. Like so many times before I concluded that God's grace is sufficient.

As the road flattened out, I was tempted to set the cruise control and give my foot a break, but I hesitated. I was worried that cruise control might push the engine too hard in the burgeoning heat. So, I kept my foot on the pedal, determined to stay in control.

By midday, hunger and fatigue set in. I pulled off the highway in Beaumont, Texas and found a Burger King where I could stretch my legs. I savored a Whopper with cheese, a generous helping of fries, and a cold Coca-Cola, allowing the cool air and the taste of comfort food revive me. I was usually frugal and health-conscious in my food choices, but the road has its own dietary conventions. After my meal, I poured over my road map and reviewed the notes I'd made, double-checking the exits I'd need to take to reach the border at Brownsville.

I hit the road again, feeling confident because my drive up to that point had been uneventful. Then I entered Houston. It came out of nowhere. One minute the highway had two lanes, then four. The city was a sprawling display of urban development. Suddenly, I was in the middle of the massive four-lane highway, with cars speeding past on both sides. I realized, with mounting panic, that I was three lanes away from my exit—the one that would take me toward Brownsville. The old Texas saying, *Everything is bigger in Texas* took on new meaning as I stared at the sea of fast-moving vehicles.

How was I going to make it across three lanes of relentless traffic? My pulse quickened as I weighed my options. Cars zipped by at breakneck speeds, leaving little room for error. Heart pounding, I flipped on my emergency flashers and stuck my left arm out the window, signaling desperately for someone—anyone—to let me over. Miraculously, a few drivers slowed down and I seized the opportunity, inching my way across the lanes. It was a nerve-wrecking, white-knuckle maneuver, but somehow I made it to the exit without causing a collision. Relief flooded through me as I merged onto the highway leading south. I took a deep breath and let go of a sigh, releasing the jolt of anxiety and the pulse of adrenaline out of my system. "I'm too old for this. Maybe I should've flew." Doubt was creeping its way up my spine. I thought about pulling over to gather my thoughts, but I kept driving.

The rest of the drive to Brownsville was smooth and uneventful, the traffic thinning as I left the city behind. By evening, I arrived at my destination and checked into a hotel not far from the border, close enough to see the bustling activity at the immigration checkpoints for both the United States and Mexico—just a thousand meters apart. As I settled into my room, the day's adventures replayed in my mind, filling me with a sense of accomplishment and anticipation for the journey still ahead.

Chapter 4

I ARRIVED AT the American Immigration checkpoint long before most travelers, only to find the gates thrown wide open and not a single United States immigration officer in sight. The silence was almost surreal and far from what I anticipated. But as I approached the Mexican immigration checkpoint, the scene changed.

Inside the booth sat two Mexican immigration officers. One of them, a woman, stepped out and called to me, "Belizean?" Her thick Spanish accent colored the word, and I replied, "Yes." I had all of my documentation at the ready in a clear plastic zip bag in my glove compartment, but without so much as a glance at my passport or travel documents, she swung the gate open and waved me through, instructing me to go ahead.

My first stop after crossing the border was for food in the city of Metamoros. I saw a restaurant and pulled into the parking lot and noted all the signage in Spanish. I hoped that my limited Spanish would be enough to get me through. I had a friendly waiter who was patient with me as I ordered my eggs, bacon, coffee, and bottled water in broken Spanish. He began to speak to me in English and told me he was happy to have the chance to practice his English. We chuckled together.

He attempted to share his history. He once worked in Brownsville before deciding to return to Mexico. We struggled to understand one another at some points. I used my AT&T smartphone to translate English into Spanish.

At the end of our interaction, he explained how I could get back to the highway to make my way to Tampico.

The journey to the City of Tampico unfolded smoothly, the road stretching ahead for about six hours. I made one pit-stop about 100 miles in at a gas station to top off my tank and check my tire pressure. I met an Asian Indian man who spoke perfect English. After a brief conversation, I hit the road once again.

My first encounter with Mexican law enforcement came at a police checkpoint. Three elite Mexican officers and a Federales policeman stood watch. One officer approached, but instead of the interrogation I half-expected, he simply opened the gate and gestured for me to pass. I nodded my thanks and continued on my way.

As smoothly as the journey was going, I needed a break. I pulled into a gas station to refuel and let my vehicle cool down. I filled the tank with Shell V-Power and noticed how the car responded—accelerating with a newfound smoothness and speed. The engine purred and I could almost hear the metallic hum of aluminum, just as the mechanic in Ferguson described. It was a reminder that my car's engine was crafted from aluminum, not steel.

Stories of Mexican bandits and drug dealers prowling the highways echoed in my mind, but still, my journey was uneventful. I pressed on and arrived in Tampico as the afternoon sun dipped low, and checked into a hotel conveniently located just off the highway.

Before dawn the following morning, I set out for the city of Vera Cruz. I believed I carefully reviewed the road map and plotted my route out of Tampico, but fate had other plans. I took a wrong exit and soon found myself lost in a maze-like neighborhood. Spotting a gas station, I pulled in and saw two Mexican taxi drivers deep in conversation. With my limited Spanish, I interrupted and explained my predicament, offering two-hundred pesos (about ten USD) for help getting back to the highway. After finishing their chat, one driver approached, accepted my offer, and motioned for me to follow his taxi.

I followed the stranger through the dark, unfamiliar streets of Tampico in the early morning and it was nerve-wrecking. I had no idea where he was leading me, and the fear of being set up gnawed at me. We wound through narrow streets and twisting alleyways. We climbed a steep hill before he stopped, got out, and pointed me toward the highway to Vera Cruz.

Contrary to the stereotypes many Americans hold about Mexicans being corrupt or opportunistic, this cab driver had every chance to take advantage of me but chose not to. He could have demanded more money in a secluded alley or at least asked for extra when we reached the highway, but he didn't. He was content with the two hundred pesos I'd given him. His honesty and decency were a powerful reminder that most people do not fit the negative stereotypes—there are so many good, genuine, and honorable Mexicans. He was a sincere human being who wanted to be helpful—a powerful reminder that God does, indeed, work through people everywhere.

As I continued toward Vera Cruz, the reality of how close I could have come to danger struck me. The possibility of being robbed or kidnapped was real, but I felt protected—as if divine intervention had placed that honest cab driver, one of His servants of peace and humility in my path. The memory of that tense but ultimately uplifting encounter soon faded into the background as the miles rolled by.

The drive from Tampico to Vera Cruz took about six hours. My legs began to cramp from keeping constant pressure on the gas pedal. I was still unwilling to risk using cruise control. I wanted to stop and stretch, but the potential dangers of pulling over on the highway convinced me to push through the discomfort.

Just before reaching Vera Cruz, I spotted a Federales officer in a fully armored uniform standing by the roadside, gripping a machine gun. A fearsome site. As I passed, he simply waved, a polite gesture that eased my nerves as I entered the city. I wondered what they were looking for and why there were federal officers located along these roads.

I checked into the Holiday Inn in Vera Cruz and arranged with the hotel staff for a trusted cab driver to guide me out of the city the next morning. The receptionist provided the driver's name and taxi registration number. The cab driver arrived at 5:30 a.m. and I followed her through the city until she pulled over, pointed to the highway leading to Villa Hermosa, and wished me well.

The drive from Vera Cruz to Chetumal—the capital of Quintana Roo, just twenty miles from the Belize border near Corozal—was the longest leg of my journey. Determined to reach the border in a single day, I passed through two toll booths, each guarded by police officers armed with machine guns. I handed over the exact toll, the bars lifted, and I pressed on. In Minatitlán, I stopped at a gas station, popped the hood to let the engine cool, grabbed a quick meal, and returned to the road.

Two more police checkpoints awaited. At first, an officer with a heavy machine gun approached as I kept both hands on the wheel. He silently inspected my vehicle, circled it, then nodded to his colleague to raise the gate. He did not even say a word to me. My heart raced and my palms sweated, but again, I was waved through without being asked for any documentation. For whatever reason the officers didn't ask for my vehicle registration and insurance, I attribute it to divine intervention. Later I would realize my ease at these check points were because law enforcement assumed I was a native headed home.

Chapter 5

THE BUSTLING BELIZE Immigration Station in Santa Elena lay just miles south of the Mexico border, adjacent to Subteniente López. At the official border crossing int0 Belize, my crisp United States passport was meticulously examined, as was my State of Missouri motor vehicle registration. A uniformed immigration official came outside to search my vehicle, but instead only asked me questions about my belongings. We went back inside the office, and she stamped with an extension, telling me that after 60 days I would be expected to register my vehicle with Belize Customs and pay the Custom's duty fee for my vehicle.

The Immigration officer exuded a warm and welcoming demeanor and inquired about my final destination within Belize. When I replied, "Punta Gorda," she smiled broadly and said, "Welcome to Belize. Welcome to Punta Gorda—it's a long way down there in the South." Her friendly words immediately made me feel embraced by the country's legendary hospitality, a hallmark of Belizean culture celebrated by travelers and locals alike.

Outside the modest immigration building, I was approached by three local men—savvy currency changers—who seemed to intuitively know that I needed to exchange my USD for Belizean currency. Belize's fixed exchange rate, set at two Belize dollars for every one USD, is a practical legacy of the country's close economic relationship with the United States, reflecting its unique position as the only English-speaking nation in Central America. This consistency makes transactions simple for visitors and highlights Belize's welcoming stance toward international travelers.

After the currency exchange, I proceeded to the small but efficient insurance office to purchase the mandatory 60-day auto insurance required for all vehicles that enter Belize. The insurance agent, a friendly and inquisitive man who had spent time in the United States, engaged me in a lengthy and informative conversation. He explained the similarities and differences between Belize's auto insurance system and that of the United States. He highlighted how Belize's regulations are shaped by British colonial heritage and the need to accommodate a diverse, multicultural population. He reiterated the immigration officer's warning that I would be expected to register my vehicle with Belizean customs at the end of the 60-day insurance policy.

The agent's curiosity was genuine—he peppered me with questions about my journey, my origins in the United States, and whether I had encountered any trouble with Mexican bandits or police at the numerous checkpoints along the way.

He insisted, "My friend, driving inside Belize is not the same as it is in the United States. Our Belizean roads are narrow, which make driving kind of dangerous. You really have to be careful, driving in Belize."

Although I could have recounted my entire drive from St. Louis through the vast and varied landscapes of Mexico to Belize, I was eager to get back on the road and reach Punta Gorda, the southernmost town in the country. I decided not to draw the conversation out.

I told the agent that my drive through Mexico had been remarkably smooth, with several police checkpoints where I was waved through without a single question. The agent speculated that the Mexican police likely assumed I was Belizean, noting that officers at the checkpoints are known to be particularly respectful toward Belizeans, especially those of Creole and Garifuna descent. This is due to the strong neighborly ties and shared history between the countries, as well as Belize's reputation for peace and neutrality in the region.

If the police realized I was an American citizen, the agent suggested, they might have searched my vehicle. According to him, my appearance allowed me to pass as a Belizean, which facilitated my journey.

I found it elucidating to speak with him because it confirmed some of my speculations regarding the inside story of how things work in Belize. After he answered my questions, I was even more interested to talk to him. He filled in the blanks for me.

At that point, I clarified that although I am a United States citizen, my country of birth is Sierra Leone, West Africa. To my surprise, the agent immediately named Sierra Leone's capital—Freetown. When I asked how he knew this, he explained that there is a prominent street in Belize City named Freetown, home to many Creoles. This detail reflects Belize's colonial past: the country was once a British colony—British Honduras, and the Creole population, descendants of African slaves and British settlers, is concentrated in the Belize District, particularly in Belize City. I was aware of the Creole community's prominence but didn't know about Freetown Street.

As our conversation continued, I learned more about the agent's own background. He proudly shared—East Indian descent, with ancestors who were brought to Belize as indentured laborers to work on sugarcane plantations during the British colonial era. This migration, which began in the late 19th century, contributed to Belize's rich tapestry of cultures, which today includes Creole, Garifuna, Mestizo, Maya, Mennonite, Chinese, Lebanese, and other communities. I was delighted that my first meaningful encounter in Belize was with an East Indian Belizean, a testament to the country's remarkable diversity.

With my paperwork complete, I set out on the scenic Belizean highway, feeling a profound sense of relief and excitement at having finally arrived in the country that would become my new home. Yet, despite this sense of arrival, I was acutely aware that I was still a stranger in a foreign land, with much to learn about its people, history, and vibrant culture.

I had 169 miles to go on the jewel of the drive: Hummingbird Highway, affectionately named for the vibrant populations of hummingbirds that are often found along the route—a trek of roughly five hours through the flat lowlands, cane fields and farmland, small villages, and stretches of sun-beaten brushland, with patches of forest and wetlands. It cut through the Maya Mountains with rolling hills, lush rainforest, citrus groves, and limestone cliffs, mist hanging heavy in the air.

I made my way to the coastal plains, dense jungle now flanking both sides of the highway. Villages of the Maya dotted the Southern Highway. To the east, there were occasional glimpses of the periwinkle blue Caribbean Sea, where it is difficult to distinguish between the skyline and the water. As Punta Gorda drew closer, the forest thickened—more tropical now. Palms and broadleaf jungle pressed right up to the roadside. The drive itself was a cross-section of Belize's geography, all in one long, scenic stretch.

~~~~

As I continued my drive south, I reflected on my first trip to Belize. I was looking forward to visiting with Ms. Vernon once again. I would later discover that Ms. Vernon had passed away prior to my return. I still had so many questions, and I was looking forward to more of her stories. The memory of our meeting—and the knowledge concerning the culture she fiercely preserved—helped me get to know Punta Gorda in a more intimate light. I count meeting such a cultural icon as a once in a lifetime blessing.

When I arrived in Punta Gorda my education on the legacies of prominent Belizean female icons continued. In the moments that I was in Ms. Vernon's presence, I witnessed firsthand the living legacy that visionary women like her and other leaders had. She touched me in a way that opened my eyes to the power of women in Belizean culture.

Myrna Manzanares of the National "Kriol" Council is yet another cultural icon that I had the honor of meeting. She is a powerful and kind woman. Through the guidance of women like her, whose impact on music, activism, and national hospitality, preserves the stories and spirit of the Kriol people, and allows the culture to continue to flourish on the shores of the Caribbean and far beyond.

Another remarkable Belizean female icon I've met is Ms. Elizabeth Zabaneh, affectionately known as Mizzab. Since I arrived in Belize 2017, I have attended Mass at a number of parishes around the country—from St. Peter Claver Parish in Punta Gorda to St. Francis Xavier Parish in Corozal—but one parish that stands out in particular is St. Pius X Catholic Church, located in the village of Mango Creek–Independence in the Stann Creek District.

One Sunday shortly after my arrival in Belize, I traveled about 60 minutes from Punta Gorda to St. Pius X in Mango Creek. I arrived approximately 15 minutes early for Mass. I wanted to be sure to get a good seat. I entered the church and made my way to my favorite spot: right in the middle aisle facing the altar. A short gentleman walked up to me, introduced himself, and welcomed me. I thanked him for his kindness.

"Where are you from? You certainly don't sound like a Garifuna or an American," he said.

I sang my familiar refrain, and I added "I am visiting St. Pius X Catholic Church, trying to get to know the surrounding areas and get to know the community."

The gentleman then told me he wanted me to meet the older woman seated at the piano to the left of the altar. I introduced myself to her, repeating my refrain.

Elizabeth Zabaneh aka Mizzab
5 Nov 1942 ---

She clasped both of my hands warmly and said, "My name is Elizabeth Zabaneh. You can call me 'Mizzab.' You are most welcome to St. Pius X Catholic Church in Mango Creek."

As I returned to my seat, a few parishioners came to greet me. A short, extremely well-dressed, bald Belizean man came forward to shake my hand and welcome me.

Later, I learned that Mrs. Zabaneh is a prominent figure not only in the church but also in the community. I came to find out that the 82-year-old matriarch runs a family grocery store and hardware store located on the ground floor of their family home. The store is an impressive establishment. She is a meticulous and spritely woman, who is immensely intelligent. She is always busy managing all aspects of the family run business: Tony's Super Store.

She is a pillar of St. Pius X Mango Creek Catholic Parish. When she enters the church, and she takes her seat and spreads her fingers at the piano, the church comes to life. She is a virtuoso pianist and her talent lifts everyone's spirits every time she plays. She is the consummate community leader. Because there is a shortage of priests in the Stann Creek District, there are only monthly visits from priests. Mizzab works with the Eucharistic Service Ministries to hold the church together between the monthly visits. The church would not be the same without this highly respected woman.

I gifted her a copy of my book *Friendship: A True Story of Adventure, Goodwill, & Endurance* though I wondered if she would have time to read it. I was delighted to have her come to me on another Sunday, before Mass, have her take me by both of my hands, and say, "I have read your book, and I love it. You have a remarkable story. God was truly looking after you. I've given your book to my daughter, Ysela, for her to read."

Mrs. Zabaneh invited me to her home for lunch with her family. I was welcomed by her son, Emilio, and his wife at the table, where we shared a traditional Belizean meal of rice and beans, meatballs, and fried plantains. During the meal, I asked Mrs. Zabaneh to tell me more about herself.

She stood and invited me into her living room, where classic family photos lined the walls. Pointing to one picture, she said, "This is my uncle, George Price, the first prime minister of Belize." There was a picture of a young man seated at a piano. "I lived with him and his family when I was a girl, and he taught me so many things, including how to play music." She went on to show me photos of her parents—her father from Wales, England, and her mother of Maya heritage—along with her siblings. I was deeply honored by her openness and hospitality.

My later research confirmed her place among the iconic women of Belize. She held a distinguished record of public service: she had served as Speaker of the House of Representatives of Belize and as President of the Senate of Belize. In addition to her musical talent, she is a former commissioner of the Supreme Court of Belize. The British Colonial title: Officer of the British Empire (OBE) was bestowed upon her by the Governor General, who represents the British

Crown. She has traveled to Britian and met Queen Elizabeth. When I asked her about those roles, she told me she was honored to serve her country. I felt a profound sense of belonging to be welcomed not only into her church but into her home. Here was this woman who had broken barriers and held two of the highest ranked political positions in the country, she made time for relationship building with a random immigrant like myself. I felt grateful to have made her acquaintance.

~~~~

Language in Belize is a living mosaic. There are a number of languages that are spoken in the country. While English is the "official" language, day-to-day in Belize, more people speak Kriol. The Kriol language is a lively English-based vernacular that is spoken by nearly everyone, weaving together influences from Africa, Europe, and the Caribbean. I have to admit that since I arrived in Belize, I have struggled to understand the language. Kriol is spoken by descendants of slaves in many parts of the world like in Nova Scotia in Canada, in the State of Louisiana, in the United States, and even in my own home country of Sierra Leone. Even though the dialect of Creole differs from region to region. Over time it has become less difficult to understand the spoken language. I believe I had to develop an ear for it.

I spent my first night as a transplant in Corozal, a tranquil town near the Mexican border. There, I observed that most residents spoke Spanish, reflecting the town's predominantly Mestizo population, and that there were few Black people in the area.

The next morning, after checking my vehicle's fluid levels and filling the gas tank, I set off for Belmopan, Belize's inland capital—a city established after Hurricane Hattie devastated Belize City in 1961. The three-hour drive took me through a landscape of short trees and savanna-like vegetation, typical of northern Belize's limestone lowlands.

As I continued south from Belmopan, the scenery changed dramatically. The vegetation became lush and dense. The trees grew tall, forming a thick, emerald canopy overhead—a hallmark of Belize's vast tropical rainforests. I knew from my research that the forest of Belize are a home to exotic animals like sleek, muscular black jaguars, the cousins of the horse and rhinoceros, tapirs, the toucans with their black feathers and their large vibrantly colored beaks, and countless other species.

As I drove further south, I began to pass through Maya villages. I saw families living in traditional thatched-roof houses on either side of the asphalt highway with power lines strung alongside the tree line. It was like seeing two different worlds living side by side.

In one village, I encountered a group of Maya mothers and their children walking along the roadside. The women balanced bundles of firewood on their heads, while the children carried water jugs. Nearby, men rode bicycles laden with firewood. I marveled over the evidence of the enduring traditional lifestyles of Belize's indigenous communities.

Approaching Punta Gorda, I saw two Mennonite men guiding a horse-drawn cart loaded with watermelons. Mennonites, who migrated from Mexico to Belize in the 1950s and 60s, are known for their agricultural expertise and distinctive dress. The men and women dress fully covered despite the heat. The men dress in blue shirts with stripes and black pants, while the women where brightly colored long dresses and head wraps. They dress their children according to gender, too. I slowed down, waved to them. Although they returned the greeting, they never stopped moving. I smiled with the children and continued on my journey.

I was so grateful for the many connections I made during my initial visit before leaving St. Louis. Keisha had agreed to do the legwork of securing a two-bedroom apartment and purchasing all the necessary appliances and furniture. Thanks to her, I arrived to find my new home fully equipped. I reached Punta Gorda on a Saturday evening and settled into my upstairs apartment overlooking the Caribbean Sea. The steady, cool breeze from the sea kept my apartment comfortable. After unpacking, I took a stroll to survey my surroundings. I found the central market where various merchants sell their wares. The market is located in the town's park near the grocery stores.

The next morning, I attended Mass at the local church. I arrived early and sat in the middle pew, watching as parishioners—many dressed in the vibrant traditional clothing of the Garifuna people—filed in. The women wore colorful, long dresses, often made from checkered materials, or two-piece outfits consisting of a skirt (*gudu*) and top (*chegidi*) in large, checkered patterns. Many women added decorative headpieces or scarves, a subtle nod to their

African, indigenous, and European heritage. While modern clothing is common, this was the time to display their Sunday best. The traditional attire remains symbolic of cultural pride, especially during community gatherings and festivals.

I felt so pleased and honored to be among these people, able to experience Mass in the Garifuna context. I was curious about what it would be like.

As Mass was about to begin, an older woman welcomed everyone and invited visitors to please stand and introduce themselves.

I was the only newcomer, so I stood and sang my familiar refrain, adding that I had arrived in Punta Gorda just the day before. "I have chosen Punta Gorda as my home away from my home in Africa," I said smiling. I wondered if anyone had trouble understanding my English, after all it wasn't Creole and I was very nervous as I spoke.

The congregation responded with warm applause and shouts of "welcome, welcome."

After Mass, before I met the priest, a group of men and women approached me, extending their hands, and invited me to a brief meeting at the rectory hall. These welcoming individuals were members of the Punta Gorda Garifuna Council Chapter. At the meeting, I felt an immediate sense of belonging, as they enthusiastically welcomed me as a new member of their community.

During our gathering, Martina Alvarez, a respected member of the Garifuna Council and a retired principal of St. Benedict Roman Catholic Primary School, shared a brief history of the Garifuna people and their ongoing efforts to preserve their language and culture in Belize and Central America. It was during this time that I learned that she volunteered her time teaching the Garifuna language to students in primary and secondary schools throughout the Toledo District.

In response to the threat of language loss, the Garifuna community, supported by organizations such as the National Garifuna Council and the Battle of the Drums initiative, has launched comprehensive programs to revitalize and standardize Garifuna language instruction in schools across Southern Belize. Beginning in 2012, these efforts have expanded from pioneering schools, like St. Peter Claver in Punta Gorda and St. Joseph RC in

Barranco, to include several more institutions in the region. The ambitious goal is to ensure that every Garifuna child has the opportunity to learn and use their ancestral language, keeping it relevant for generations to come.

This Garifuna's passionate cultural revival stands in sharp contrast to the fate of some other indigenous groups in Belize. For example, the Yucatec Mayas of Northern Belize speak Spanish as the dominant language, as they have largely lost their native language due to colonial pressures and cultural assimilation. However, inspired by the Garifuna's example, there are emerging efforts to revive and teach the Yucatec Mayan language.

The Garifuna story is remarkable not only for its survival but also for its ongoing fight against extinction. The United Nations Educational, Scientific and Cultural Organization's (UNESCO) recognition of Garifuna language, dance, and music as a "Masterpiece of the Oral and Intangible Heritage of Humanity" underscores the global importance of their cultural legacy. Through the combined efforts of grassroots activists, educators, and cultural organizations, the Garifuna people are not only safeguarding their language but also inspiring a broader movement for indigenous language preservation throughout Belize and beyond.

While some indigenous languages in Belize have been nearly erased by the tides of history, the Garifuna continue to stand as a beacon of resilience and cultural pride. Their unwavering efforts to teach, speak, and celebrate their language ensure that the Garifuna identity will endure, echoing through the voices of new generations and the classrooms of Southern Belize.

The Garifuna people were the early educators in Belize. They were mostly teachers who traveled throughout the country to teach in primary schools. One such teacher, Dr. Ludwig Palacio, reports having to walk miles to teach Maya children in the villages of the Toledo district.

Even though the Garifuna people were the early educators in Belize, sadly today, the Garifuna people are disproportionately under-represented in official government positions and education employment numbers.

Having established myself in Punta Gorda, I was approached by a respected local figure—Mr. Wil Mahea. Mr. Mahea is a prominent Garifuna leader and the Coordinator of efforts concerning Belize's territorial waters and the ongoing land dispute over the Sarstoon River with neighboring Guatemala. He invited me to join him and a lively group of Belizeans on an expedition to the disputed waters of the Sarstoon. It was an invitation fraught with both historical significance and present-day tension. Despite the honor of being asked, I politely declined involvement in what was both a deep, local and intensively, international conflict. At that time, I still considered myself an outsider, not yet fully naturalized in Belize.

Nevertheless, my curiosity grew. I immersed myself in learning about the turbulent history surrounding these territorial disputes. My research revealed a pivotal truth: Britain's long shadow still darkened land and water struggles between Belize and Guatemala. Both countries, once under British colonial rule, carry colonial legacies that have continued to shape their destinies.

One of the British Empire's well-worn tactics was "divide and conquer"—a policy made chillingly clear at the infamous Berlin Conference of 1884–1885. At this gathering, European powers carved up the African continent, with not a single African representative present to speak on behalf of their own land. This blueprint for partition was later echoed in the drawing of arbitrary borders throughout the British Empire—including Central America. Such imperial lines have sparked enduring conflicts from Africa to South Asia and the Americas.

As someone born a British subject in pre-independence Sierra Leone, I felt compelled to delve deeper. I listened to the unwavering confidence of local Belizeans in Punta Gorda, who insisted that Guatemala had absolutely no legal grounds to claim Belizean territory or its turquoise coastal waters. Time and again Belizeans invoked a series of colonial-era treaties—most notably the 1859 Anglo-Guatemalan Treaty, in which Britain and Guatemala agreed upon borders that, in the view of Belizeans, should have forever settled the question. Yet Guatemalan authorities have periodically claimed all or part of Belize, even including it on official Guatemalan maps and in classroom curricula, keeping the dispute alive for over five generations.

Today, the fate of this dispute rests in the hands of the International Court of Justice (ICJ) at The Hague. Throughout Belize, from the lively markets of Belmopan to the quiet lanes of Punta Gorda, patriotic Belizeans express optimism that the ICJ will affirm their claims. Many speak passionately of Britain-backed documentation—treaties, official correspondences, and colonial-era records—that purportedly reinforce Belize's sovereignty.

But history is not just written in treaties and political proclamations. My visits across the region—traversing from bustling Guatemalan towns to the lush rainforests of Honduras—revealed another truth. The people living on both sides of the border are united by deep familial, ethnic, and cultural bonds. The Garifuna, whose roots stretch across Belize, Guatemala, and Honduras, remain bound by their ancestral language, pulsating drumming, and shared memories of migration and resilience. Likewise, the Q'eqchi' and Mopan Maya of Belize trace their bloodlines and traditions across both borders, with villages like Jalacte, Dolores, and Crique Sarco serving as living bridges. These borderland residents move freely to visit loved ones, attending ceremonies and family gatherings unhindered by the invisible lines set by colonial mapmakers.

On the banks of the Sarstoon River, a place where Guatemalan patrol boats and Belizean Defense Forces often face off with tense formality, I could not help but think of other contested frontiers. The Sarstoon, steeped in tropical greenery and echoing with the calls of exotic birds, conjures images almost as tense as the Korean Demilitarized Zone, or the snow-capped valleys of Kashmir. Yet there is a key difference: while those other borderlands are policed by mighty armies bristling with tanks, Belize's Defense Force is a small, dedicated corps—young men and women committed to peace but dwarfed by Guatemala's more formidable military. Belize has no standing army, and its entire population is smaller than many world cities—a fact which underscores both its vulnerability and its remarkable resolve.

The borders between Belize and Guatemala are porous, almost conceptual. Despite language differences and official checkpoints, the social and cultural tapestry remains seamless. Garifuna families share recipes and stories across miles. Mayan festivals spill from one country into another. Even the waters themselves—fresh and salt, river and sea—pay little heed to international agreements.

When I hear my Belizean friends confidently declare they will emerge victorious at the ICJ, I sometimes wonder how much they understand of the complexities of international law. The first step for the ICJ will be to nudge both parties toward negotiation—a process that could take years of diplomacy and compromise—far from the jubilant optimism found on the street, and if the parties can't come to a compromise then a full litigation will ensue, and, in the end, the court will render its final decision and judgment, which may or may not be in favor of Belize. Aside from politics, what truly stands out is the intricate web of human ties that defy simple borders. Whether or not treaties, courts, and governments recognize it, the people of Belize, Guatemala, and Honduras remain forever intertwined—by ancestry, by culture, and by a shared stake in the future of this extraordinary corner of the Caribbean.

Chapter 6

MEANWHILE, AFTER I settled in Punta Gorda, my memoir
Friendship: A True Story of Adventure, Goodwill, & Endurance that I wrote with the
initial goal of paying homage to Tom Johnson, my benefactor, became a fire
starter. I achieved paying homage to Tom and more. When I first published
my book, I recognized that the book would not simply sell itself. The reality
for self-published indie authors is quite different; we must become tireless
promoters, creative marketers, and relentless advocates for our own work.
Upon publication I was determined to share my story, I promoted my book
through interviews in newspapers, on radio, and on television. I did not pay an
exorbitant amount of attention to my book. I was satisfied with the exposure
and the five-star reviews on Amazon, Goodreads, and Barnes & Noble from
readers all over the world. I expected to only share my book within my social
circle, but my online reviews come from hundreds of people who I do not
know.

I began to seek out collaborators for my film project. After my screenplay,
Diamond of Hope, was written, I subscribed to IMDB-Pro, a media program that
contains the names of current Hollywood film producers, directors, agents,

Reviewers of my book found my story inspiring, with the potential to
make a significant positive impact on humanity. Many reviewers commented
that my story read like a film. Because of the nature of my life-changing story
and its potential to make positive impacts in the world, I decided to adapt my
book to a character study screenplay, in hopes that I could share my story with
more people.

media and represented media publicists for actors, executives and studios. I read through each of the agent's pitch and query letter requirements. Because I am African American and my story involved a white man who transformed my life from poverty in Africa to opportunity in America, I began to pitch liberal and African American producers, directors, agents, executives and studios. I sent query letters to Oprah Whinfrey's O Productions Studios, sent query letters to Tyler Perry Studios and to his representative agents. I sent query letters to DeVon Franklin and his media agents and publicists. I sent query letters to Dr. T.D. Jakes and to his representative agents. I sent query letters to Appian Way Studios (a production company owned by Leonardo DiCaprio) and to his representative media agents and publicists.

I sent query letters to the most popular liberal media executives, their agents, their represented media publicists, and I never heard from any of them. I made an earnest effort and followed up with numerous phone calls to the production companies and the agents of all these outlets. My phone calls were ignored and in the few instances when someone answered, I was told that, "we do not accept unsolicited calls and scripts."

I was not deterred. I found out that one of my favorite books: *Same Kind of Different as Me* by Ron Hall and Denver Moore, published in 2006, endorsed by Barbara Bush, had been adapted into a screenplay and movie in 2017. The similarities between the story of the black homeless man, Denver Moore, and his white benefactor Ron Hall's friendship and the relationship I'd formed with Tom Johnson were striking. Hall firmly believed that the privileged have a responsibility to extend compassion and sympathy to homeless people. After meeting Moore, Hall refused to leave him to a fate of hopelessness. Hall called Moore a friend and made it his mission to travel around the United States to advocate for the homeless everywhere, working in shelters and soup kitchens.

Sadly, Denver Moore passed away before the film was produced and shown in theaters, but Ron Hall was still living and working. I found Ron and began to dialog with him about the connections between our work. We shared the impacts 0f our life-changing experiences of forming unlikely friendships across cultural boundaries based on faith and the belief in empathy and shared humanity. We exchanged numerous emails and began to promote one another's work. After reading my screenplay he helped present my work to producers he knew. Likewise, I promoted his film named after the book he collaborated on with Moore and Vincent within my readership.

Because of the Christian aspect of my story and screenplay, I joined Christian Filmmakers, Christian Producers, and Christian media Facebook Groups, and I began to pitch my screenplay on these Christian filmmakers' Facebook pages.

Because of the redemptive nature of my story, people who took interest in my story and pitch were Conservative Christian media people. To wit, I joined a Facebook group called "Redemptive Media" and the administrator of the group was a Christian woman named Dr. Diane Howard. When I found out Dr. Howard is a Media Journalist and Editor of a Christian Magazine, I messaged Dr. Howard and pitched my screenplay and story to her. This proved to be a serendipitous connection.

After Dr. Howard read my queries and my posts about my story and screenplay, she gave me her personal email and told me to send my script to her. Within two days, Dr. Howard read my script. She liked my story so much that she got back to me within two days and voluntarily wrote the concept and synopsis of my screenplay. Normally this service would cost a considerable amount of money to have someone of Dr. Howard's talent and caliber to complete for me. Yet another example of how God works through people. Dr. Howard blessed me with a tool I would need to take the next step in my journey.

As if the tool she gave me wasn't enough, Dr. Howard gave me her personal information and asked me to call her. When we spoke, she volunteered to be my *pro bono* advocate. She truly liked my story. Dr. Howard told me she would take my screenplay "upstairs," meaning she would present my screenplay to top prominent producers, directors and executives in the Christian film industry. She has functioned as my *pro bono* advocate for my screenplay since 2019 and continues to the time of this writing to work tirelessly to bring my vision to light. During her interviews she tells the producers and directors she interviews about my story and screenplay.

Dr. Howard presented my story and screenplay to a gentleman named Brian Bird. Brian Bird is the producer and director of the award winning and successful television series "When Calls the Heart" featured on the Hallmark Channel. Through Dr. Howard, Brian Bird read and critiqued my screenplay and concluded that, with minor changes, my story is timely in America and is a good fit for the big screen.

Next, Dr. Diane Howard presented my story and screenplay to Dr. Ted Baehr, the President of *Movie Guide* in Hollywood. Dr. Baehr read my screenplay, and he presented it to Christian production directors. Meanwhile I continued to pitch my screenplay on Christian Facebook pages.

I was pitching my screenplay in one of the Christian filmmakers' groups when I came across a gentlemen named Marc Whitmore. When I researched Marc, I found out that he is a prominent media creation and distribution executive for ORI International, a media creation and worldwide distribution of films. I also found out that Marc is also President and CEO of MWO Management Company, with Offices in Hollywood, CA, London, England, and in Dubai, UAE. I pitched my screenplay to Marc. He gave me his email and told me to send him my script. Within a few days, Marc responded saying, "Francis, this is a good script." I was delighted.

After about three weeks, Marc reached out letting me know he had presented my screenplay to his team. He told me, "It will take them few months to look at it, so be patient." This was my first sign of real traction. I prayed for patience every day, sat back, and waited. I felt lucky that a prominent Christian media executive had taken interest in my screenplay. Ultimately, he said he wanted to meet in person.

I flew out to Hollywood. In all my years in the United States, I had never been to California. From the time I landed at the airport I was in awe. I was well traveled, but little that I'd seen up to that point had prepared me for Los Angeles. I took a cab from LAX to Sunset Boulevard. The atmosphere was electric: there were luxurious cars and everyone looked like stars.

Mr. Whitmore and I had plans for lunch. As we drove, he pointed out buildings and Hollywood landmarks. I saw Hotel California, where the Eagles recorded the famous album by the same name. As we pulled into Beverly Hills I was further amazed at the luxurious cars and the people in outrageous, colorful clothing. I felt dwarfed by all the bright lights in the big city. Being in the heart of Hollywood was an adventure and will forever be tied to my memories of getting my film produced.

The changing landscape in the film industry, due to the challenges and aftermath of the pandemic, the strikes in the film industry, and the impacts of

AI, have all made independent film production a daunting task. Much like money can't buy you love, a great screenplay script doesn't necessarily mean that you'll go right into production. I had the love I just needed the money to take the next step.

My initial expectation was that I would get picked up by liberal outlets, but I actually found my greatest audience among people like my benefactor, are conservative Christian people. This said to me that much like Tom's interests and ultimate love for me, support and community transcend race and national origin. Dr. Diane Howard, Marc Whitmore, Dr. Ted Baehr, Brian Bird, and Michael Landon, Jr. devoted their time and resources to presenting my project and fundraising. Their interest has spurred me on, encouraging my passion and validating my pursuit of the goal of getting my story to the big screen.

Even if my screenplay is never produced into film because of the challenging landscape in the industry, I consider it a victory and a success because my story and screenplay impacted these prominent media authorities in the Christian Media Industry who took interest in it, who took their time and resources to advance my script, without charging me a penny. I consider it a success because the experience of having these people, from a completely different background and world, seeing a universal Christian connection to my story was a life-changing experience. They took my work higher up and brought it to the brink of it being produced, which by itself is an accomplishment that so many self-published, indie authors never experience.

~~~~

Belize's immigration and naturalization process is refreshingly straightforward compared to the labyrinthine bureaucracy of the United States. I'd already taken my vehicle to the Belize Customs Office and paid the fee to be allowed to register my vehicle with the Belize Motor Transport Department. I'd swapped my Missouri license plates for Belizean plates after the 60-day waiting period, and I traded my Missouri driver's license for a Belizean license. As an American citizen in Belize, I had been reporting monthly to the local immigration office to pay a $50 BZD fee for my visa extension. After a year of this ritual, I was finally eligible to apply for permanent residency—a milestone that felt both momentous and surreal.

My application for permanent residency was not a solo endeavor. The Garifuna community of Punta Gorda, who had embraced me as one of their own, stood by my side. On the day of my permanent residency interview at the Belize Immigration and Naturalization Service office, I was accompanied by two pillars of the Garifuna community: Margaret Castillo, a compassionate retired nurse, and Dr. Ludwig Palacio, a renowned Garifuna intellectual, author and artist. Dr. Palacio, whose life's work spans veterinary medicine, painting, and authorship, owns a local art gallery that pulses with the colors and rhythms of Garifuna heritage.

Both Margaret and Dr. Palacio were interviewed and signed "Affidavits of Character" in support for my residency. Their unwavering support echoed a pivotal moment from my past—forty-three years earlier, at the American Embassy in Palermo, Sicily, Italy where my benefactor, Tom Johnson, vouched for me with a heartfelt affidavit. His words, steeped in conviction and history, opened the door for my education in America. I remember my friend and benefactor Tom Johnson's response to the United States Embassy consul like it was yesterday. He said, "My name is Thomas Johnson. I have never voted for a Democrat. I am a decorated Vietnam war hero with two Purple Hearts and a Distinguished Flying Cross. I have a conservative Christian background. My great grandparents were Presbyterian Ministers who built the first church in Bloomington, present day Minneapolis, and worked with the Dakota Indians. I am here today to sign an affidavit of financial support for Francis Mandewah. He was a poor boy I met in Sierra Leone who was desperate for education. I sponsored his primary school education, and now I am here to sign affidavits to sponsor his college education in the United States. I am currently employed as chief pilot for Viking Helicopters of Canada with a 10-year contract with the World Health Organization in Africa to treat and prevent the disease of river blindness in four West African countries. I have my military awards papers with me, and I also have my current pay stubs and bank statements if you wish to see them."

I am certain that Tom's intentions, will, and resources convinced the American Embassy consul to issue the visa that allowed me to live in America.

In Belize, the moral character references provided by Margaret Castillo and Dr. Ludwig Palacio were as powerful as Tom's affidavit had been decades before. Their testimonies to my character and contributions were instrumental in my successful residency application.

With permanent residency granted, I felt compelled to give back to the community that welcomed me so warmly. Drawing on my experience as a retired probation and parole agent, I became a volunteer counselor for at-risk youth at Toledo Community College. The school library became my sanctuary where I met with students identified as struggling with behavioral challenges. Each session was an opportunity to inspire, to listen, and to help shape brighter futures.

At an earlier date I'd sought out Dr. Vincent Palacio, President of the University of Belize after Mass one Sunday at St. Peter Claver Church in Punta Gorda. I approached him and introduced myself and offered him a copy of my book. He offered to meet me at a restaurant where we discussed the possibility of an Adjunct Instructor teaching position in Public Administration. He told me to keep him informed, and after my permanent residency was granted, I submitted my application for a part-time instructor position at the University of Belize.

~~~~

Five years passed in a tapestry of service and belonging. When I became eligible for Belizean citizenship, Margaret Castillo and Dr. Ludwig Palacio once again stood by my side, accompanying me to my citizenship interview. Despite my confidence, I was acutely aware of my status as a foreigner and the possibility of rejection.

During the interview, both character sponsors were asked why they supported my application. Their response was a chorus of acceptance: "Mr. Mandewah has become part of our Garifuna family. He is of good moral character, volunteers as a youth counselor, is a prominent member of St. Peter Claver Parish, and serves on the Garifuna Council. Punta Gorda is his home, and we are his family."

I was then interviewed in a separate room by another immigration officer during which I was asked a number of questions as to why I wish to become a

Belizean citizen and what contributions I would make to Belize. I reiterated my desire to continue working in service to help the at-risk youths at Toledo Community College.

I became an active member in my parish in Punta Gorda. After a meeting with one of the priests, I was completely shocked to find out that the St. Peter Claver Parish, my spiritual home in Punta Gorda, is a Jesuit parish under the administration of the Diocese of St. Louis, Missouri—my former home in the United States. The interconnectedness of these communities, stretching from Missouri to Belize, filled me with awe. What was the likelihood of such a coincidence? I could not help but feel that the hand of God was guiding me.

I felt guilty for not letting Fr. Rosebourough of the Blessed Teresa Calcutta parish in Ferguson, Missouri know that I was coming to settle in Punta Gorda in Southern Belize. I now felt an obligation to telephone him and let him know about my overland journey to Belize through Mexico, and my membership in a new parish in Punta Gorda. I called his cell phone. He recognized my voice immediately, which felt good. He asked me how I was doing and in a hesitant voice, I told Fr. Rosy I was doing fine. I told him I was calling to apologize, confess, and to surprise him in a positive way.

"Tell me all about it, Francis…you are an interesting guy."

"Father, I am calling you from Punta Gorda, a town in Southern Belize, in Central America. Father, I should have let you know the last time you saw me at mass that I was preparing to leave St. Louis to drive my vehicle through Mexico to Punta Gorda, where I have decided to retire and settle."

Fr. Rosebourough asked me how my trip was, driving through Mexico to Belize. I explained to the priest that God was on my side. I traveled through Mexico without incident, and I arrived safely in Punta Gorda.

To my surprise Fr. Rosebourough stated, "Francis, the parish in Punta Gorda in Southern Belize is under the Diocese of St. Louis here in Missouri. In fact, Francis, I know the Bishop of Belize, Rev. Lawrence Nicasio went to seminary right here in St Louis, so you found a home church away from your home church here in Ferguson. When you see Bishop Nicasio, tell him Fr. Rosy in St. Louis says "hello." God bless you, Francis. I will let the parishioners here know you are in Belize. God bless you. Take care."

Our conversation, filled with warmth, surprise, and the enduring bonds of faith touched me. I felt a surge of gratitude for the connection that I felt.

My next phone call was to Sr. Rosanne to let her know I safely made it to Punta Gorda. I knew she had been waiting to hear from me. I was certain she had prayed for me to complete my solo mission, driving through Mexico. Unfortunately, when I called the SSND Provincial Home St. Louis, MO to speak to her, I was told that she had traveled to Ghana for organizational meetings with the SSND sisters in that country. I left a message to let Sr. Rosanne know that I had safely arrived and settled in Belize in a town called Punta Gorda.

A few months later I called her cell phone, and I was so happy to hear her voice. She recognized my voice. "I got your message about your safe arrival. You are truly blessed," she piped up. "How was the driving and how many days did it take you to arrive in Belize?"

I narrated the whole journey with stops in Jackson, Mississippi, in Tampico and Vera Cruz.

"Francis, you are an amazing adventurer. God was looking after you. I said prayers for you. I'm glad that you made it to Belize without any problems. Stay in touch, God bless you."

I felt a warm place in my heart for my connection to this Catholic nun, who had been a spiritual friend and mentor for the better portion of my life.

I continued to seek to satisfy my curiosity about the diverse culture in Belize. The Toledo District, lush and untamed, is home to more villages than any other district in Belize. The ancient traditions of the Q'eqchi and Mopan Maya thrive, their languages and customs echoing through the rainforest. Living among the Chippewa Ojibwe Native American Indians in Hayward, Wisconsin for several years gave me an opportunity to develop a special fondness for and a curiosity about Native American peoples and their cultures. I was now ready to interact with and experience the Maya people and learn more about their culture.

My initial foray into these communities took me to villages on the way to the Guatemala border. The first Maya village that I visited was the village of San Antonio, a Mopan village and first Maya village that was established in the Toledo District. Every Sunday, I drove from Punta Gorda to attend Mass in the village's spacious church to attend the Maya Mass. The presiding priest, an American migrant and I were the only non-Mayans. The church was filled with lots of children. This warmed my heart to see the young so attentive to spiritual matters.

Barranco is a small village located approximately twenty miles south of Punta Gorda. It is home to around 120 people. It was the first Garifuna village that I visited. While the village is situated on the coast, I had to drive through a number of Maya villages in the inland area, including Santa Rosa, Santa Ana, Midway and more, before I finally arrived at Barranco.

The journey itself was an adventure—rough gravel roads flanked by towering Mahogany trees, stretching between the village of Midway and Barranco, a testament to Belizean natural wealth.

My 2003 Hyundai Elantra GT finally pulled into the village of Barranco, where I was greeted by a Garifuna gentleman named Egbert Valencio, who would later become a good friend. In our introduction, I shared by common refrain, detailing my origin story. I explained that I had specifically driven to Barranco because I had read that it was exclusively settled by Garifuna people, and I felt a deep interest in their culture and traditions—especially since they reminded me of my own village in Sierra Leone.

Egbert took me around the village and introduced me to each and every household. They all received and welcomed me warmly. At one point, I sat down with Egbert and had a longer conversation with a Garifuna family. An older lady in the home spoke to me in the Garifuna language, which is a melodic blend of West African and indigenous words. She encouraged me to repeat what I heard her say in Garifuna. I struggled to pronounce what I heard her say in Garifuna. They all laughed at my mispronunciations, thinking it was quite funny. "It's time that you learn how to speak Garifuna," the matriarch said.

As much as they were impressed with my efforts to learn to speak the Garifuna language, they were equally curious to know the name of the language that my people speak in my village in Sierra Leone, which is Mende. It was a wonderful cultural exchange moment for me.

The Garifuna's pride in their heritage was palpable. With their West African, Carib, and Arawak people's ancestry, they are renowned for their music, dance, and storytelling. Preservation of culture is important. The woman spoke passionately about preserving Barranco's simplicity.

In my encounters and conversations with Belizeans, who speak mostly the Creole language, I continued to listen attentively to the words and their pronunciations in order to grasp their meaning and understand what was being said.

I had to listen attentively to understand what the woman was telling me about her village of Barranco. "We want Barranco to remain as it is—small, pristine, with no tourism here. We are poor. We don't need the pomp and materialism of tourism here. We have our land where we grow our food. We have the sea where we fish. We don't want what happened to the Garifuna village of Seine Bight to happen to us," she explained.

I wondered what happened to Seine Bight, but I didn't ask her. It did pique my curiosity, and I knew I would have to find out for myself.

Suddenly, the old lady changed the subject and asked if I had ever tried the Garifuna specialty dish called *hudut*, a traditional coconut milk–based fish stew served with mashed plantains.

When I responded that I had not, the lady joked and said, "Well, we have to get you a Garifuna wife then!"

As I navigated the winding road toward Punta Gorda, the landscape transformed around me into a lush, emerald world. Towering, ancient trees arched overhead, their branches weaved together forming a living canopy that filtered the sunlight into shifting, golden patterns on the ground below. The thick, humid air was fragrant with the scent of earth and blooming flowers, and the chorus of tropical birds and distant howler monkeys filled my ears. The vibrant jungle reminded me vividly of the dense forests of my childhood village in Sierra Leone, where I once followed my mother—our village's only herbalist—on her sacred quests to harvest roots, bark, and petals for healing.

After settling into the gentle rhythms of Punta Gorda, I made my way one morning to the lively fish market by the sparkling seafront. There, amidst the bustle of fishermen and the salty tang of the sea, I noticed a slender black woman perched on a wooden stool behind a modest table. Her table was a miniature apothecary, covered with an array of herbal roots, barks, dried leaves, and twigs—some bundled in twine, others preserved in tall glass jars. The sight pulled me in, stirring memories of my mother's careful hands sorting through similar treasures.

Curious, I approached and began to examine the herbs, letting my fingers brush over the rough textures and earthy scents. I picked up a bag of finely ground powder, holding it up for her to see. I held it in front of her, and I asked her what it was for. She greeted me with a radiant smile and stood up, her eyes sparkling with warmth.

"This is for a female condition called fibroids," she explained. "But these ones here are for men," she added, pointing to a dried, gnarled root sealed in a clear jar. "This is for men's prostate conditions." Before I could ask more, a tourist approached, seeking advice. I stepped aside, content to watch as the herbalist shared her wisdom with another seeker. I learned that the herbalist's name was Meridette Martinez.

Once her customer departed, Ms. Martinez beckoned me closer with a wave of her hand. She apologized for the interruption, then continued her patient tour of the table, naming each herb, bark, petal, and root in Garifuna and describing the ailments they were meant to heal. Her knowledge was encyclopedic, her passion unmistakable. The table itself seemed to glow with the wisdom of centuries-old traditions.

She looked up at me and asked if I was searching for something specific. I confessed that I was simply drawn in by the memories her herbs, which evoked memories of my mother, the healer of our African village.

Ms. Martinez's eyes lit up with interest. "Where in Africa are you from?" she inquired. I repeated my origin story, and she replied, "Oh, so you're one of us now."

She welcomed me warmly, her voice full of genuine curiosity. "Please, tell me more about your mother who was the herbalist in your village. I am very interested to hear about her herbal knowledge if you remember."

I described how, in a world without clinics or pharmacies, my mother's wisdom was our lifeline. We would venture into the forest at dawn, pickaxe, machete, and hoe in hand, searching for healing plants. My mother could identify every species—trees with deep taproots that required hard digging, flowering vines whose petals she would gently pluck, and bark she would carefully scrape from tree trunks. She knew how to dry, grind, and mix these gifts of nature into remedies for fevers, wounds, and mysterious ailments. As I spoke, the market faded away, replaced by the memory of cool forest shade and the rhythmic sound the tools made as I would dig the roots up for her.

Ms. Martinez listened intently, then asked, "Is your mother still alive?"

I shook my head "no" and explained that my mother's knowledge was never recorded—none of my family could read or write, and I was away when she passed. Her herbal legacy, so rich and vital, was lost upon her passing.

Ms. Martinez sighed, her face clouded with understanding. "It is unfortunate that none of your mother's herbal knowledge was recorded," she said. "I am trying to pass on my herbal knowledge to our young Garifuna generation, but, unfortunately, they are not interested. The young Garifuna think it is old-fashioned to be an herbalist, and I try to explain the spiritual and economic aspect of having herbal knowledge to the young generation but to no avail."

I nodded, feeling the weight of her words. "Yes, I absolutely agree with you, especially about the economic side. The natural herbal supplement industry is huge in the United States."

Ms. Martinez snapped her fingers, her eyes alight with conviction. "Yes, my brother, we do know that almost all of the active potent ingredients in the herbal supplements on the shelves sold in the Western world come from tropical rainforests like the one we have right here." She gestured broadly to the misty silhouette of the Maya Mountains, rising majestically behind Punta Gorda.

I smiled, recognizing the truth in her words. When I first visited American health food stores, I was amazed to see so many herbal supplements sourced from plants that grew in the rainforests of Sierra Leone. The Western world's billion-dollar wellness industry is built on the ancient wisdom of indigenous healers—wisdom that is at risk of vanishing as younger generations turn away from these traditions.

As another customer approached, I thanked Ms. Martinez for her time and wisdom. I left the market feeling both nostalgic and grateful—grateful to have met a kindred spirit who reminded me of my mother's legacy, and fortunate to live in a place where the rainforest's bounty is still within reach. The air was thick with the scent of herbs, the promise of healing, and the hope that, somehow, the old knowledge will survive, carried forward by those who cherish it.

On my way back to Punta Gorda, I decided to get to know more about the tourist's side of southern Belize. I became curious about the state of the village of Seine Bight that the woman in Barranco mentioned. Like the herbalist's practice, was it a place where there was a fusion between natural resources and modernity or something else?

Located on the Placencia Peninsula, Seine Bight is located near one of the more expensive tourist destinations in Belize. Even though Belize is mostly rural with villages and towns, to the outside world Belize is known as a paradise for tourism with exotic beaches and resorts. I was disappointed to find that that the village of Seine Bight is the poster child for villages left behind by resort development.

About two miles before reaching the village, I could see multi-million-dollar mansions, bungalows, and resorts lining both sides of the peninsula. When I finally arrived in Seine Bight, I immediately noticed the stark contrast: on one end of the spectrum is the village itself, which is rife with extreme poverty, and on the other end of the spectrum the coastal community surrounded by luxurious homes owned by foreign expats and tourists.

It became apparent to me why the old lady in Barranco wanted Barranco to stay as it is—simple and pristine—without the tourism. Modernity doesn't necessarily mean prosperity for the locals. In fact, places like the resorts are built by and for the rich, and with all the tourists traffic the rich simply get richer and the local poor get poorer. It is a juxtaposition that underscores the tension between tradition and modernity that defines much of Belizean life.

Another rich and relevant tourist stop is the village of Monkey River a small fishing village located on the Caribbean Sea. Access to the village of Monkey River is both by boat and highway coupled with a trek along a rough, gravel road.

As is indicated by the name Monkey River, there are monkeys in the thick tropical forest on the way to the village of Monkey River. I was grateful for the aluminum engine of my 2003 Hyundai Elantra GT on the rough, gravel road without fear of damaging parts of my vehicle. I drove very slowly, so it took me almost an hour from the highway to finally arrive in the village of Monkey River.

The gravel road is flanked by thick tropical rainforest. As I moved along slowly, I could hear monkeys howling in unison. I was so intrigued that I pulled to the side of the narrow road to stop and listen. Once the howling subsided,

I began to see the branches of high trees shaking and the closer I looked, a vision of monkeys springing between branches came into focus.

I was familiar with the sight of monkeys from my youth in Sierra Leone, but I noticed that the monkeys of Belize looked different from West African monkeys. These had smaller bodies and ears with shorter tails.

When I finally arrived in the village of Monkey River, I saw approximately 15 houses made out of wood along with a few concrete houses. The locals there are mainly fishermen and there are tourist resorts nearby where they offer jungle excursions.

To the outside world, Belize is generally considered a tourist bastion, complete with exotic beaches and islands that cater to the largely affluent American, Canadian and European foreigners. I visited a number of Belize's tourist bastions, though they didn't impress me as much as the tourist destinations in Italy and Greece. During my tenure in Europe, before I came to America, I frequented the famous Greek Islands of Mykonos and Crete, where the spectacular blue Mediterranean Sea offers European tourists the most exotic vacation beaches. It's fair to say some of Belize's vacation destinations, especially on the Ambergris Caye Islands, remind me of the sandy beaches along the blue Mediterranean Sea in the Peloponnese of Greece where I worked as a migrant farm worker picking olives, oranges, and mandarins before I moved to the United States in 1984. The beaches on the Placencia Peninsula reminded me of the beaches along the coastline of Reggio Calabria in Southern Italy where I lived with the Italian Staganelli family. The Placencia beachfront also reminded me of the blue Mediterranean Sea beach in the Sicilian Town of Taormina. The more sights I see, the more I recognize a synergy to the landscape and construction of tourist locales everywhere. People from all over the world seek out the beauty of beaches and ancient architecture. They wish to experience native cultures replete with their tastes and sounds.

Not that I've never worn the hat of a tourist and ventured into tourist locales, but I am much more interested in the authentic cultural experience brought by exploration of off-the-beaten-path areas and immersion into native cultures. While tourism is an important part of the financial strategy for Belize, I don't believe that the typical tourist experience carries the charm and depth of exploration of the countryside and simple villages.

Since Belize gained independence from the United Kingdom in 1981, the country has steadily become a magnet for expatriates seeking a blend of natural beauty, affordability and a slower, more meaningful pace of life. Belize's English-speaking environment, friendly and multicultural society, and welcoming residency programs have contributed to a steady influx of foreign residents, particularly from North America and Europe. While expatriates often form their own supportive communities, many also integrate with local Belizeans, participating in cultural festivals, community events, and the daily rhythms of village life, creating a dynamic and inclusive atmosphere.

Placencia's rich tapestry of cultures is the result of centuries of migration and settlement. The area was originally settled by the Maya people around 2000 BC, as evidenced by archaeological sites indicating at least 14 ancient settlements around the Placencia Lagoon, primarily established for salt production and coastal trade. These settlements underscore Placencia's early importance as a center of commerce and culture in the region. In the 17th century, English Puritans from Nova Scotia and Providence Island arrived and established a small community. Though their settlement was short-lived, dissolving during the Spanish American wars of independence in the 1820s, they left a lasting legacy in the area's name: Spanish explorers called it "Placentia," and the location became known as Punta Placentia, or "Pleasant Point."

Between the late 1800s and early 1900s, Placencia became home to five pioneering Belizean Creole families who built their livelihoods through fishing. As these families grew and prospered, the village expanded, welcoming new residents and evolving into a thriving community. Just up the road in Seine Bight, a Garifuna settlement flourished, and, over time, more Garifuna people began to settle in Placencia as well, bringing with them their vibrant traditions of drumming, dance, and storytelling.

The first Chinese immigrants arrived in Belize in 1865 as indentured laborers following the abolition of slavery. While many initially worked on sugar plantations in northern Belize, some eventually moved south. Political changes in Hong Kong and mainland China coupled with Belize's citizenship-by-investment program launched in 1986 brought a new wave of Chinese migration. Today, Chinese families in Placencia operate grocery stores, restaurants, and other small businesses that are now integral to the local economy.

Chapter 7

WITH ITS EASY access to the Cayes and the bounty of both the sea and the land, Placencia is an attractive place to vacation, live, and work for both national and international peoples. The village's growth has drawn even more Belizean Maya and Mestizos, who are attracted by the opportunities offered by the thriving tourism and fishing industries. The resulting vibrancy of cultures—Maya, Creole, Garifuna, Chinese, Mestizo, and expatriate—makes Placencia an endlessly fascinating place to call home.

Among the many tourist bastions I have visited, one of the most interesting is the village of Placencia, a picturesque settlement at the end of a long, slender peninsula that stretches gracefully from Maya Beach in the north to the southernmost tip, lying adjacent to the twin villages of Mango Creek and Independence on the mainland. Access to the mainland is a 14-minute boat ride on a Hokey Pokey water taxi, which departs every two hours from either direction. The village of Placencia is just south of Seine Bight at the end of a long road, made longer by a generous application of speed bumps. The peninsula itself is a remarkable natural wonder, bordered on one side by the tranquil, wildlife-rich Placencia Lagoon and on the other by the sparkling turquoise expanse of the Caribbean Sea, whose gentle waves caress miles of pristine, powdery white sand beaches. The lagoon is a sanctuary for manatees, crocodiles, and countless species of birds, while the sea, protected by the second-largest barrier reef in the world, is alive with vibrant coral gardens, schools of tropical fish, and the occasional pod of playful dolphins. The area's unique geography, with its easy access to a constellation of small, palm-fringed islands known as Cayes, has made Placencia a magnet for adventurers, nature lovers, and those seeking a tranquil escape.

I found a way to insert myself into the marketplace at Palencia. I met people from all over the world, and, in the course of conversation, I would mention my memoir, *Friendship: A True Story of Adventure, Goodwill, & Endurance*, which I wrote and self-published in the United States in 2016. One afternoon, a Canadian man struck up a conversation with me and I found myself embracing the role of my own best salesman. His interests was piqued and he asked how he could get a copy. I told him that I had physical copies at my home in Punta Gorda, but he could also download it for Kindle. He promised he would. When I returned to Punta Gorda, I kept having flash backs of the conversations with the Canadian expatriate. In conversation with the Inn keeper, Mr. Charles, he suggested that I promote my book and share my story amongst the tourists. It was in Belize, and specifically in Placencia, that I discovered the perfect location to meet my audience face-to-face.

Placencia, with its steady flow of American, Canadian, and European travelers, provided an ideal setting for me to showcase my printed book and sell it directly to readers. These travelers, often arriving in droves from cruise ships or flying in to stay at the luxurious beachfront resorts that line the peninsula from Maya Beach to the heart of the village, brought with them a curiosity and openness that made every encounter rewarding. Yet Placencia is not merely an exotic tourist destination; it has also become a cherished home for a growing community of expatriates from America, Canada, and Europe. These individuals, drawn by the allure of a relaxed and simple lifestyle in a pristine, natural environment, have chosen to extricate themselves from the rigid, fast paced, and materialistic lifestyles of the West, seeking instead the peace and authenticity that Placencia offers.

~~~~

I awakened to the cheerful tunes of the Yellow-Tailed Oriole and the Great Kiskadee, whose songs repeatedly call out their own names. The sun rose, bringing with it a gentle warmth. At its zenith, it would make us sweat, move slower, and speak in mellow tones, with the morning air still fresh and filled with the chatter of birdsong. In that lull before climbing out of bed, I stretched and considered the coming day, planning to sell my book in Placencia. Breathing deeply, I caught the scent of my neighbor's cooking—there was no mistaking a fresh fish fry with Creole spices crackling in the pan. My stomach growled in reply. That made up my mind: today I would get some fish at the pier. I liked to position my table near the pier to share my book. It was the perfect place to reach tourists arriving on cruise ships. Often, I left by 2 o'clock, but I had heard that the fishermen came in with their catches after 4. That day, I decided I would stay a little later to get some fresh fish.

After a successful day of book sales that left me feeling satisfied, I packed everything up and wandered over to the pier to sit and enjoy the view of Placencia Point. I enjoyed watching all the children along with a few adults, playing in the beautiful blue green water while awaiting the boats that were sure to come. And then they came. First one, and then many. Fishermen arrived at the dock with boats laden with the freshest catch, selling from the boat or unloading it to the pier to be sold in other locations. Locals and restaurant owners select from an array of seafood that changes depending on seasonal availability and the rhythms of the sea. The fish are ready to be taken home as they are, or scaled, gutted or filleted by the fisherman for a small additional price.

Fishing has long been central to Placencia's economy and culture. Coastal Maya settlements have fished in these waters for thousands of years. Within the last two centuries, various groups—especially the Garifuna and Creole—have continued the tradition, sustaining families through fishing. Traditional methods like handlines, traps, and canoes were once the norm.

As I sat on the pier, I spied a smaller boat drifting toward me. It contained an elderly Garifuna man, his skin weathered from years at sea. He saw me watching and hailed me from his motorboat.

"What is your favorite fish?" he asked.

"Red Snapper!" I replied without hesitation.

"And your second favorite?" he continued.

"Well, I guess shrimp," I said. "But that's a hard call—I like shrimp quite a lot, too."

He laughed with me. "I very much agree, sir. I also love shrimp!"

He explained that his favorite way to cook shrimp was on kabobs with fresh pineapple, red pepper, onion, and some seasonings—so delicious over coconut rice. My mouth started to water. Even though I had fish on my mind when I arrived, I ended up buying the shrimp; nothing is more delightful than shrimp directly off the boat.

I found out his name was Aranda. He apologized for not having caught any red snapper that day but promised his son, Chagua, would likely bring some the following day. Just as I was paying, Chagua walked up.

"I'd like you to meet my son," the fisherman Aranda said. "He is a master fisherman and boat captain. He has incredible luck spearfishing because he's such a fast swimmer and knows exactly where to find the catch."

I looked up to see a tall, middle-aged Garifuna man, with a swimmer's body, a quick smile, and a friendly demeanor. We struck up a conversation immediately, like old friends.

Before long, they were regaling me with their best fish tales, each more fantastic than the last. I was fascinated. I had known Belize's barrier reef was abundant, but perhaps not to this extent. Talking to these men, whose lives revolved around the sea, made every description vivid. I had spent time in the Mediterranean in Greece, but I am more a landlubber than a sea-going creature. Still, their accounts of fish, coral, sea mammals, and invertebrates captivated me.

The Garifuna are renowned for their maritime traditions. Descended from West African survivors of a shipwreck and indigenous Carib islanders, they arrived on Belize's southern coast in the early 19th century. Fishing is more than an occupation—it is integral to Garifuna identity. Boys learn to fish from a young age, often using hand-crafted dugout canoes and nets passed down through generations. The sea provides food, income, and spiritual inspiration. Garifuna cuisine celebrates fresh seafood, with dishes such as *hudut* (fish in coconut sauce) and *sere* (fish soup). Community and sustainability are core values, with traditional conservation methods helping maintain balance with nature.

After our conversation, Chagua invited me on a motorboat ride the next day. Someone had hired him to go out, so it was easy to include me. He had legal permits to take people fishing and snorkeling. He even had extra gear for me to use, so I could tag along with no costs to me.

I met him at first light near the Hokey Pokey water taxi dock in Placencia. He and the man who hired him were loading gear onto the boat: snorkels, long fins for free diving, normal-length fins for me, some spears, and strange clear tubes closed at each end.

Curious, I asked, "Could you tell me what those tubes are for?"

As we motored north, he explained: "I'm not a professional scientist, but I consider myself a citizen scientist. About 40 years ago, someone released captive lionfish into the ocean from an aquarium. They have venomous spines and are not native to Florida or Central America. They multiply rapidly and eat many native fish, disrupting the ecosystem. To remove them, we spear the lionfish and carefully place them in these tubes, preserving the natural balance while avoiding stings. I've spent time learning about this process for quite some time. Having someone with the permits to show me the proper way to harvest these fish is a life goal of mine."

Chagua added, "While we spear lionfish, there'll be plenty of opportunities for you to snorkel and watch the reef." I had seen pictures of lionfish, but I didn't realize how much they threatened the marine environment. It was sobering to think about how one careless act could create such widespread ecological problems.

People often do not understand the consequences of their actions. At one point, I remember hearing that Pan-American Airlines, in conjunction with the Guatemalan government, decided to introduce black bass to Lake Atitlán in Guatemala. They were hoping to increase sport fishing opportunities to draw more tourists and help the economy. Unfortunately, the bass fed on the small fish and crabs, and within a few years had cleared out two-thirds of the native species. The little fish that lived in the lake were the food of a rare bird species called Lake Atitlán grebe. That particular bird was emblematic of the culture of the Maya people who live around the lake, appearing throughout their art and crafts. In a very short time after the introduction of the bass, the grebe was declared extinct due to food scarcity. Nature exists in a fragile balance that humans too easily disrupt.

Our destination was Southwater Caye Marine Reserve. I was told this place was incredibly biodiverse and a real natural treasure. But it does have a lionfish problem. So, they have to regularly cull lionfish in this area with pole spears. Southwater Caye is a great example of Belize's commitment to preserving one of the most beautiful and biologically diverse marine environments in the world, while actively empowering local communities and visitors to protect it for generations to come.

I was told that this was a perfect place to snorkel because there was a shallow reef we could go to that teemed with life. The water was crystal clear, and I might see anything from parrotfish to angelfish, barracuda, rays, and maybe even a dolphin. I was curious and just a little nervous. I wasn't sure whether I should be worried about sharks, but they told me the sharks in this area were not dangerous. If anything, it would probably just be a nurse shark, which was not aggressive.

After a long boat ride of about an hour and a half, Southwater Cayes finally came into view. We got our gear on—wet suit, fins, googles, oxygen tank, and mouthpiece—and jumped in. Immediately, I was overtaken by awe. Such a profoundly different view from above the water to under the water. The surface did not reveal the profound explosion of life beneath its calm exterior. Swimming in water that was about 9 feet deep, I looked down on corals of all descriptions—soft corals moving with the waves, sturdy brain corals and branching corals abounded. There were more kinds of fish than I could possibly identify. But I did recognize the French angelfish with its shades of gray and that very distinct turquoise line delicately framing the end of its tail. Enormous yellow pork fish swam on by. Gorgeous purple fan corals undulated in the waves as the ghostly presence of an eagle ray floated by. I felt a certain sense of astonishment as I swam through a cloud of thousands of sardines glittering with a silver rainbow light as they passed all around me. I was struck by the majesty of God's creation, and I felt such a profound gratitude for the gift of this world and this life.

I swam over to where the men were hunting for lionfish. Triggered spears are not allowed in the marine reserve, so I got to watch their hunting skills as they carefully aimed from as close as possible to thrust their pole spears into these marine interlopers. I can see now how those tubes were essential because you certainly wouldn't want to touch those spines. After a time, we loaded back onto the boat to move to our next destination.

The captain dropped a few lines into the water in hopes of catching a few fish as we continued south to Placencia. Almost before I knew it, one of the lines was hit by some kind of fish. After a little bit of a struggle, he reeled in one of the most beautiful red snappers I've ever seen.

Chagua said, "This one is for you, my friend. I know it's your favorite."

That evening, as I feasted on perfectly cooked snapper, I found myself reflecting on the wonders of Belize's barrier reef—the second largest in the world. I now understood why this underwater sanctuary draws visitors from every corner of the globe: it is more than a destination, it is a living, breathing marvel. I drifted to sleep with the lull of the ocean in my ears, grateful for the day's adventure, the camaraderie of new friends, and the incredible beauty hiding just beneath the waves of Belize.

~~~~

Since setting up my small mahogany table by the sidewalk next to the Tourism Police booth at the pier, I've had the pleasure of meeting countless tourists and vacationers who stop to browse my memoir. The inspiring and captivating nature of my story often piques their curiosity, especially when they learn that I wrote and self-published the book and that the cover features my own photo alongside my friend and benefactor Tom Johnson. Some buyers quickly relate to my story after reading the blurb on the back, which highlights a direct connection to the Hollywood film *Blood Diamond* starring Leonardo DiCaprio. These personal interactions are deeply rewarding; I autograph each purchased book and take photos with the tourists and their families, making every sale a memorable and meaningful experience.

Given the inspiring nature of my story, I traveled throughout Belize where I met with librarians and donated my book to their libraries. I visited the island of Ambergris Caye in San Pedro, where I met a librarian and donated a copy of my book to the San Pedro Public Library. On the mainland in Corozal, I met with the librarian and donated another copy. I also met with the administrator of Corozal Community College and donated a copy there, and I later visited the librarian at the Punta Gorda Public Library to contribute a book. Because of the inspiring and motivating message of my book for Belizean schools, I appeared on Love FM's Morning Television News with Ernesto Vasquez, where I discussed its relevance to Belizean students.

Many tourists arrive in Placencia by flying directly from their home countries to Belize City and then on to Placencia, where they stay in the luxurious beachfront resorts that line the peninsula, from Maya Beach to the village itself and even out to the exclusive island resorts. While my primary goal has always been to sell more books to the diverse array of tourists and vacationers who visit Belize from around the world, I have found that the one-on-one conversations and exchanges with these visitors are often more fulfilling and enlightening than the financial rewards. Each interaction broadens my worldview and, I hope, enriches the perspectives of those who engage with me and my story.

Placencia has provided a unique opportunity to meet and interact with individuals and nationalities from every corner of the globe. One such memorable encounter was with Anthony Fulmes, a Canadian expatriate permanently residing in Placencia. I first met Anthony Fulmes, a Canadian expatriate who now calls Placencia home, on a balmy evening at one of the village's lively social clubs. Anthony struck me immediately as a friendly and approachable man, quick with a smile and eager to strike up a conversation. We found ourselves seated at the same table, and, as is often the case in such places, our conversation soon turned to our backgrounds and the winding paths that brought us both to this vibrant corner of Belize.

"So, where are you from originally?" Anthony asked, leaning in with genuine curiosity.

"I'm from Sierra Leone, in West Africa," I replied, watching for his reaction. The effect was immediate and electric. Anthony's eyes widened, and he sat up straighter, clearly surprised.

"You're from Sierra Leone? I was there with the United Nations Peacekeeping Forces. We were the ones who finally helped bring an end to the rebel war over diamonds."

For a moment I was stunned. "What? Are you serious?" I exclaimed, unable to hide my amazement. "What are the odds that I'd meet a Canadian Army Captain who served in the peacekeeping mission in my own country—right here in Placencia, of all places? It really is a small world!"

Overcome with emotion, I reached out and shook Anthony's hand firmly with both of mine. "Thank you," I said, my voice thick with gratitude. "Thank you for your bravery and your service. You helped bring peace to my country after years of horror—the war over diamonds, where even young boys were forced to commit terrible crimes."

Anthony nodded, his expression turning somber as he recalled his experiences. I leaned back in my chair, eager to listen as he began to share his story in vivid detail. He spoke of the tense and dangerous days he spent in Sierra Leone, describing the chaos and uncertainty that defined the mission.

At one point, his voice grew quieter as he recounted a particularly harrowing episode. "There was a time when I was captured by the rebels," Anthony said, his eyes distant as if reliving the memory. "They blindfolded me and held me for what felt like an eternity. I had no idea what would happen— if I'd be tortured, killed, or maybe just left to rot. It was the most terrifying experience of my life."

He paused, taking a deep breath before continuing. "But by some miracle, I was released. To this day I have no idea why. And you know what? I went straight back to the field. I couldn't abandon the mission. I kept working with the warring factions, urging them to lay down their arms and come to the negotiating table. That's what peacekeeping is about—never giving up, even when it seems hopeless."

Listening to Captain Fulmes, I was filled with admiration for his courage and perseverance.

"You have no idea how much your work meant to people like me," I told him.

"My own village, Punduru, was right in the heart of the diamond zone, on the boundary between the Kenema and Koidu Districts. The rebels destroyed everything—homes, lives. My mother and sisters, along with the rest of the village, had to flee into the mountains, where they hid for years until the war finally ended."

Anthony listened intently, and in that moment, a powerful bond formed between us—two men from opposite sides of the world, connected by the shared tragedy and hope of Sierra Leone's civil war. That evening we became fast friends. A few days later, Anthony surprised me by visiting my book table at the pier, where I was selling my memoir to tourists and vacationers. This time, he arrived in his full Canadian Army United Nations Peacekeeping uniform, the blue beret and insignia a striking reminder of his service. He greeted me warmly, and after supporting my book with a purchase, we took a photograph together—me, the grateful author, and Anthony, the stoic peacekeeper.

Once again, I thanked him for his heroic service, knowing that his efforts, and those of his fellow peacekeepers, had helped bring an end to one of the darkest chapters in my country's history. That meeting in Placencia, under the Caribbean sun, was a reminder of how the most unexpected encounters can forge the deepest connections and bring healing across continents.

Placencia, with its breathtaking natural surroundings, rich history, and dynamic blend of cultures, stands as a testament to the enduring appeal of Belize—a place where people from all walks of life come together, drawn by the promise of adventure, connection, and the simple joys of life by the lagoon and the sea.

Placencia is not the only place in Belize where expatriates have found a home. I personally know Europeans, Canadians, and Americans who have chosen to live in remote villages among the indigenous Yucatec Mayans in north Placencia and among the Mopan and Q'eqchi' Maya in the lush, mountainous jungles of Toledo in Southern Belize.

While some people travel from other places in the world to retire in the tourist bastions in order to spend their days and nights drinking themselves into a stupor, there are many others who choose a more natural lifestyle in tune with the land and the people.

For example, Gloria Velka and her husband Jimmy, originally from Arkansas, live among the Yucatec Maya in a remote village of Xiabe where they raise sheep and goats, producing milk and cheese that Gloria sells at the Corozal market every Friday. Her cheese, reminiscent of the Greek feta I enjoyed while living in Greece in the early 1980s, is a delicious reminder of the blending of cultures that defines Belize.

Another example of the melting pot that is Belize can be found in London native Joann Audinett whose husband is a Q'eqchi Kekchi Maya. She considers herself an immigrant who has fully assimilated into the Belizean Maya culture and is involved in the local village community events and lives in the dwellings among the Mayas with her husband and two sons. This is in stark contrast to the European expats who live in their mansions and bungalows away from the locals.

Thirty-six years prior to the time I began writing this account, farmer Christopher Nesbitt, a transplant from New York City, began the job of restoring degraded land in Belize. He developed an Agro–Silvo-pastoral system where food production and environmental conservation co-exist. He has been named one of the *Leaders of Rurality of the Americas* by the Inter-American Institute for Cooperation on Agriculture.

Interestingly, Christopher Nesbitt does not consider himself and his wife, a Mestizo further adding to the melting pot of Belize diversity. He considers himself an immigrant in Belize.

As far as Chris is concerned, the term "expat" is for people who have left their country of origin but still see themselves as outsiders. They often come to places like Belize to create a lifestyle of privilege and separation from the existing culture. They do not live among the locals. They keep to their mansions and bungalows. To him, the word connotes wealthy foreigners. Because he lives in the jungle among the natives, he considers himself an immigrant—not an expat.

~~~~

After I'd been settled in Punta Gorda for a time, I remember a day when the enchanting rhythm of drumming lured me beyond my doorstep. Early one evening, as the sky transitioned from its periwinkle blue to a burnished gold, I heard the unmistakable pulse of drums and the laughter of dancers drifting from the direction of the central park. Drawn by the communal energy, I wandered over and found a bubbling crowd gathered under the open sky. At the heart of it all were three drummers, their hands working in seamless harmony. A man with long, striking dreadlocks stood out; his mastery over his instrument was unmistakable. His drumming was a mesmerizing display of skill and dexterity, each beat commanding both respect and attention.

As soon as the performance reached an interval, I made my way over, eager to express my admiration. I shook the master drummer's hand, commending him sincerely. He looked me in the eye and gave a knowing smile, his energy as warm as the tropical night.

When the event finally ended and the crowd began to disperse, he sought me out, extending the connection.

I introduced myself, singing my common refrain telling my origin story.

He gave my hand a firm shake and introduced himself, "My name is Emmeth Young," and gestured to his wife beside him. "This is Jill," he said, as she gave me a friendly, welcoming smile—her fair skin contrasting beautifully with his, further revealing the cosmopolitan nature of the community.

I was genuinely delighted to meet both Emmeth and Jill, but I was particularly intrigued by Emmeth's story. I was curious about his musical journey and the roots of his drumming expertise. Soon, Emmeth and I sat down on a low wall nearby, the echoes of the drums still lingering in the air. Although his conversation ranged from a passionate discussion of West African music and politics, my curiosity over the variety of instruments he had mastered and the breadth of the music he performed came to the fore.

Emmeth shared, "I'm a Creole from Gales Point Manatee, and my specialty—the instrument I'm truly a master of—is the Sambai Corter Base Bottom Drum. Of course, I play plenty of other instruments too. There is a fertility dance named after my favorite drum, the Sambai."

That piqued my curiosity further, and I asked if he had ever performed with the illustrious Ms. Leela Vernon, a name synonymous with the spirit of Kriol music in Belize.

Emmeth beamed. "Oh yes—she was an amazing composer, choreographer and dancer. She formed the dance group Ebolite, spreading Kriol culture and music. She's the one who gave Belize its Kriol national song, *Brok Don*. I toured with her in so many places—Europe, London, throughout the United States, even Mexico and South America. She is truly legendary."

She did a lot to promote eco-cultural tourism. She sought to integrate exploration of the intersections of local cultures and tourism. She saw appreciation of the natural areas of Belize as central to conservation efforts, economic progress, and cultural understanding. I was honored to know this true inspiration to culture and the arts. I then asked if he felt he was carrying on Ms. Vernon's legacy.

"Absolutely," Emmeth jumped to his feet and replied with conviction. "I work closely with the Ministry of Culture, teaching and inspiring Kriol youth, exposing them to our music and traditional instruments. It's so important that they know where this music comes from."

He made a cupping gesture in the air with his ample hands as if rubbing the sides of a drum and went on to reveal another side of his artistry. "I also learned how to make drums from different local woods—mahogany, cedar, mango, coconut. Each tree brings a different sound, a unique pitch and rhythm, making the drums incredibly versatile."

Though Emmeth's main focus is Kriol music, he also participates in the annual Garifuna Battle of the Drums, joining fellow musicians in embracing the spirit of unity that defines Belize's national celebrations.

As our conversation wound down and I prepared to leave, I felt grateful to have met Emmeth and Jill. Such genuine people sharing their passions are the hallmark of Belizean community. Walking away from the park that night, the memory of Ms. Leela Vernon was palpable—a poignant reminder of how her legacy endures, living on vividly through her students and disciples like Emmeth Young.

During my first days in Punta Gorda, I longed to meet someone from the African continent. I knew it was likely—legends circulated about Ms. Vernon offering refuge to newcomers arriving by boat—but I'd yet to cross paths with another person of African origin.

So, I asked a trusted Garifuna friend and neighbor if he knew of anyone. He told me there was indeed an African gentleman in town named Nana Mensah and kindly passed along his number. I dialed the number and as soon as Nana picked up his accent unmistakably revealed his African roots.

Still, I didn't know precisely from which country he hailed. Eager for connection, we agreed to meet at a local restaurant a few days later. When we finally sat down together, an easy, animated camaraderie sprang to life, and we quickly found ourselves engrossed in a long conversation about journeys, belonging, and the shared spirit of the diaspora.

As we spoke, Nana revealed his story: "I'm from Ghana," he said, bringing a flash of joy to my face, given my own years spent in northern Ghana before the long, arduous journey across the Sahara. Nana's story took an unexpected turn.

"Thanks to strong diplomatic relations between Ghana and Cuba, I was able to travel from my home to Cuba for my studies. I completed both my Bachelor of Science and my Master of Science in Agriculture and Engineering in Havana."

After finishing his education, Nana took another bold step, finally journeying to Belize, where he made an impressive mark. "Now, I work as Chief Executive Director at Belize Organic Family Farming," he explained—a role that has left him highly respected in the community. Nana's story is remarkable not only for his academic and professional achievements but also for the family and cultural ties he has further woven into Belize. He is married to a Kriol woman, perfectly illustrating Belize's identity as a true cultural melting pot.

Our meeting was not just a chance encounter; it was a meaningful opportunity to bond, to exchange stories of resilience and adaptation, and to find fellowship as Africans living far from our original homelands. That night, I felt a deeper sense of belonging in Punta Gorda, grateful for the open arms and open hearts that welcomed me, and aware that our stories—Emmeth's, Nana's, and mine—had become part of the living fabric of this joyful, eclectic place.

~~~~

Since arriving in 2017, my vehicle underwent a number of preventative measures and repairs that left me with four red lights on the dashboard signaling to check the engine. The ABS system was disconnected, so its red light glared on the dashboard, along with brake warning lights. Despite this array of scarlet warnings, the vehicle never developed a problem. Thank goodness.

I am an especially cautious driver. Having driven throughout Belize— from Corozal to Punta Gorda, from Belize City to San Ignacio—I witnessed firsthand the dangerous driving habits on the roads. I saw vehicles roll through stop signs without pausing, and I narrowly avoided several near-accident situations. A month after I arrived in Belize, my fears became reality. On the southern Highway near Punta Gorda, a drunk driver slammed into my vehicle. I had been driving toward town when a car coming from the opposite direction veered into me. Thankfully, the impact struck the driver's side doors rather than the front of my car. Had it been head-on, I would not have survived.

That near-fatal accident brought to mind the warning an East Indian insurance agent had given me: driving in Belize can be dangerous. From that day forward, I adopted a new mindset for my own safety. I began assuming that every other driver on the road was operating with a learner's permit. This perspective forced me to take extra caution and never assume that another driver would know—or follow—the rules of the road.

The rising cost of gasoline threatened to encroach on my travels around the countryside. My neighbors recommended that I convert my fuel source on my Elantra from unleaded gasoline to butane fuel. I set out on a mission to find someone to do the work.

My search introduced me to the Mennonite communities—descendants of German-speaking Anabaptists who settled in Belize in the 1950s, seeking religious freedom and land. The Mennonite community in Belize is a world apart, both visually and culturally, from the bustle of Belizean towns and the rhythms of Creole, Mestizo, and Garifuna life. Arriving in 1958 from Chihuahua, Mexico, the first Mennonites settled in Spanish Lookout, hacking their way through dense rainforest to create what would become some of the most productive farmland in the country.

Today, Mennonites number between 12,000 and 15,000 in Belize, living in tight knit, largely self-sufficient communities across the country's districts. Renowned for their industriousness, their impact on Belize's economy cannot be overstated. Their farms supply most of the nation's eggs, chicken and dairy, and their workshops produce much of the country's furniture and agricultural machinery. Mennonites are the backbone of Belize's agriculture and engineering. Yet to speak of the Mennonites as a monolith in Belize is to oversimplify a tapestry of communities, each with its own history, dialect and approach to modernity.

My first real interaction with a Mennonite community happened due to my need for their special expertise. I sought out Peter Crone, a Mennonite patriarch with a mechanic shop in the Mennonite settlement community of Shipyard of Orange Walk District, to install a butane tank in my car.

The Crone family's workshop was a hive of activity, with sons and daughters working side by side repairing machinery and running farms. Peter, a patriarch with a gentle yet authoritative demeanor, asked about my life in Africa and America, sharing in turn stories of his family's journey and their deep faith.

In all my years in the United States, I never personally met a Mennonite person. I had observed the Mennonites in their carpentry shops and farms in Wisconsin and Pennsylvania, but I never had the opportunity to interact with them. They always maintained their distance from the general population. Belize gave me the opportunity to connect and interact with them. I drove to the Mennonite community of Shipyard and met with the Crone family who own an elaborate mechanical shop where they repair heavy farm machinery and vehicles of all types.

When I pulled up to their mechanic shop, I was met by one of the sons of Peter Crone. I introduced myself and let him know that I wanted to have a butane tank installed on my vehicle. This older son, who is an expert in installing butane tanks on vehicles, came out and inspected my vehicle. He told me my Hyundai vehicle is a good fit for butane use. He explained the new technology, parts, and engineering that is involved in the installation of butane on vehicles. The costs for the parts and labor are dear, but it is an investment worth making on used vehicles because butane engines run cleaner and faster. The cumulative costs of high-priced unleaded gasoline eclipsed the costs of the adaptation.

I made a partial payment to order parts, with instructions to return in three days. When the day of installation arrived, I had to wait for five hours while the work and testing were completed. While I waited, I had the opportunity to have a conversation with the owner, Mr. Peter Crone himself. Mr. Crone was inquisitive after hearing my origin story.

Mr. Crone began his conversation by saying, "So you are from Africa? Could you please tell me about Africa? You see, I don't know much about Africa because I don't watch television; I don't listen to the news. Our lives are simple. We raise our children. We work. We care for our families, and on Sundays we go to Church, then return back to work again on Monday."

I was surprised that Mr. Crone admitted that he and his family do not watch television. I was unfamiliar with the tenets of the Mennonite way.

I began telling Mr. Crone that I come from a small village in a country called Sierra Leone. I explained that in my youth there was no electricity and no running water in my village. Everyone in my village was poor, which meant that I came from a poor family. I explained to Mr. Crone that even though my country is very rich in diamonds, my people are still poor.

Then Mr. Crone asked, "how did you get out of Africa to come to America"?

I was happy to tell Mr. Crone how I met the American pilot Tom Johnson, who was employed in the diamond mines in my hometown region and how I met him and benefited from his help with my education in America. To this day my heart swells with gratitude for Tom's kindness. In my heart and mind his kindness is connected with God's grace and mercy, so thoughts of my education and immigration still move me to tears of joy.

As much as Mr. Crone was curious to know about me, I was also very curious to know more about him. I listened wide-eyed as he disclosed that he fathered three sons and two daughters who are all married and have families of their own. His three sons married, had children, and found work together in the mechanic shop repairing farming equipment, tractors, and bulldozers.

Mr. Crone explained that his daughters and their husbands farm cattle and run grocery stores, selling fresh meat, chicken, milk, eggs, and cheese. He came across as very friendly, and I felt honored to have met him and spoken with a Mennonite patriarch.

After the installation and the road test were complete, I was advised on the maintenance and cautionary measures I needed to follow in order to avoid mechanical problems. I was told to make sure that my radiator was filled to the top with high-grade coolant, because the technology relied on abundant coolant to function properly. Keeping the radiator in good condition was essential, since my vehicle was now engineered to transition from gasoline to butane while in motion.

After I filled the 12-gallon tank with butane, I expressed my thanks and said goodbye to Mr. Crone and his family. I put my foot to the pedal and smoothly rolled out of the Crone mechanical shop. I immediately felt an unusually smooth acceleration and could barely hear the exhaust muffler, even with the windows open. My vehicle ran beautifully after the alteration.

Since the butane adaptation in 2019, I have driven my vehicle throughout Belize—from Belize City to San Ignacio, from Corozal to Punta Gorda—and had no problems, though I've kept a close eye on the radiator to make sure it is always filled to the brim with coolant.

I had another opportunity for a cultural exchange with a Mennonite patriarch. I met Mr. Walter Fritzen at the marketplace in the village of Independence, where he came every Friday morning with his wife, adult children and grandchildren to sell fresh eggs, raw milk, pork and vegetables. I arrived late one morning to buy some of Mr. Fritzen's eggs, but by the time I got there, he had already sold out. I asked him to reserve two dozen eggs for me the following Friday and offered to pay in advance.

Mr. Fritzen replied, "No, no, my friend. Hold your money. I will make sure you have two dozen eggs next Friday."

He looked at me curiously and asked, "Mister, where are you from?"

I laughed and said, "Aha! Did you notice something?"

He nodded. "Yes, because you speak English differently. Are you from America?"

I looked into his blue eyes and long white beard and said, "Take a guess. Where do you think I am from?"

He narrowed his eyes and said, "Africa?"

I snapped my fingers and replied, "Yes! You are correct. I am from Africa, but I am also an American citizen."

"So, you came from Africa all the way to Belize?" he asked.

I explained briefly that I came to live in Belize because I liked the country and its people, and that it was an honor to meet him, a Mennonite. Then I asked him to tell me about himself.

"Sure," he said, stretching his arm out to point to his adult sons, grandchildren and great-grandchildren. "Those men over there are three of my 10 adult children. The three next to them are my grandchildren, and the little ones you see there are my great-grandchildren. Let me tell you something—I was the very first Mennonite who came to Belize to settle. We Mennonites are farmers. I raised all my children on the farm. We have cows, chickens, goats, pigs, and we grow different kinds of vegetables. We work hard. We maintain our families, and on Sundays we go to church."

The more interactions I had with Mennonites, the more I realized they held a strong Protestant work ethic. They devoted nearly all their time to work.

I was impressed by Mr. Fritzen's eloquent English, so I asked where he had learned it. He said that when he was a young man, he lived with a Mennonite family in Pennsylvania, where he learned English.

We enjoyed discovering things about each other, though he was busy with his family. Before leaving, Mr. Fritzen invited me to his farm to speak again. He also maintained a grocery store where he sold fresh meat, eggs, and more. I told him I would stop by his store in the village of Red Bank.

It took me half an hour to drive the dusty, bumpy gravel road to the village of Red Bank, where Mr. Fritzen and his family lived.

The Mennonite community of Red Bank is generally considered more traditional and conservative compared to some of the larger, more modernized Mennonite settlements. While there is significant diversity among Mennonite communities in Belize with each developing its own distinct character, Redbank stands out for its adherence to a simpler, more insular lifestyle. For example, the Red Bank Mennonites are more likely to restrict the use of electricity, modern machinery, and vehicles, relying instead on horse-drawn buggies and traditional farming methods. This contrasts with progressive communities like Mr. Crone's up in the Orange Walk district, where cars, tractors, electricity, and even cell phones are commonly used. Red Bank Mennonites also maintain a more conservative dress code, with men and women wearing plain, modest clothing reminiscent of 19th-century European peasant attire. In fact, women typically sew their own garments and wear prayer coverings in public. Men can buy their clothes, but they must still adhere to strict guidelines.

Red Bank Mennonites primarily speak Plautdietsch (a low German dialect) among themselves, use standard German for church and school, and speak English or Spanish only when interacting with outsiders. Education and religious instruction are tightly controlled within the community, emphasizing Bible study. Like other conservative Mennonite settlements, Red Bank is tightly knit and inward-focused, with social life revolving around the church and communal activities. Marriage outside the faith is rare, and the community strives to minimize outside influences to preserve their religious and cultural identity. Red Bank Mennonites maintain a traditional lifestyle that emphasizes simplicity, self-sufficiency, and separation from modern society. When I visited Red Bank, I was able to see much of this firsthand.

Mr. Fritzen came out of the store and kindly welcomed me as his wife watched. I browsed the modest store and chatted with the owner. I selected fresh cheese, milk, and eggs, and after a bit of brief conversation, I paid for my items and waved him goodbye. I drove back home giddy, having deepened my connection with yet another part of the community of my new home. Because in Wisconsin the Mennonites did not interact with the outside population, I never had the opportunity to befriend anyone, so I was delighted that I made connections with the Mennonites in Belize and gained insight and experience into their ways of life. I was impressed by their quiet modesty, deep commitment to family ties, and their work ethic.

My next mission—to make connections and gain insight into the world of the Maya in Toledo District.

Chapter 8

ALTHOUGH MY HEART was captivated by the vibrant rhythms and soulful traditions of the Garifuna people, once I found my footing within their warm, welcoming community, my curiosity expanded. I yearned to immerse myself in the rich tapestry of Belize's other ethnic groups—especially the ancient and enigmatic Maya of Southern Belize. In the past, I found exploration of indigenous groups incredibly enriching. Having spent two transformative years living among the Ojibwe Chippewa on their reservation in Hayward, Wisconsin, where I absorbed the deep-rooted customs and spiritual traditions of Native America, I knew that true understanding could only come through direct experience. To truly grasp the living history of the Maya, I needed to meet them face-to-face and wander the sacred grounds of their ancient cities, as well as going to the villages and meeting the people of modern-day Maya culture.

I read and heard tales of the legendary late classic Maya ceremonial and political centers. These archaeological wonders, shrouded in the mists of time, once thrummed with religious rituals and political intrigue. Eager to witness their grandeur, I set out on a journey through the lush, emerald heart of Southern Belize. On my way, I stopped in the small, sun-dappled village of Indian Creek, where I asked a local man for directions to the ruins. The gentleman was friendly and eager to help.

He told me, "It's about half a mile from here to the Lubaantun archaeological site."

When I asked if he was a resident, his eyes shone with pride as he replied, "born and raised in Indian Creek."

I introduced myself, explaining that I was originally from Africa, now an American citizen, who chose Punta Gorda as my place of retirement.

Our conversation blossomed into a lively and informative exchange as I asked about the history of his village. He began, his voice resonant with ancestral pride, "Well, you are on your way to experience for yourself the Maya historical sites at Lubaantun and Nim Li Punit, which will show you that my culture and traditions have survived for hundreds of years—and we are still here. This is my village. We live in tune with nature; we have our land, our rivers and streams. We grow our food, raise our chickens, goats, pigs, and lambs. We build our houses with timber and thatch roofs and live in them today just as our forefathers did centuries ago."

I listened, captivated, as he continued to weave the story of his people's resilience and connection to the land. He looked at me with knowing eyes and said, "Well, you are from Africa, so you know about the impacts of colonialism."

I nodded, replying, "Yes, I am fully aware of the effects of colonialism, the havoc that the colonists caused on the continent of Africa." I had a great deal of direct experience of it, growing up near the diamond mines where people from outside of my country came in and took away valuable stones, leaving or sharing almost nothing with the people who actually lived on the land.

His voice grew somber and passionate. "My friend, colonialism never ended. It is still continuing, but in different forms."

Curious, I asked him to explain how colonialism persisted in the present day here in Belize.

He answered, "The government wants to take our land away from us Maya. This is our ancestral land, belonging to us and our future generations. But right now, all the Mayans in the Toledo District have taken the government of Belize to court, and to the United Nations, to fight for our rights to keep our land."

As I absorbed his words, he shifted the conversation.

"Did you hear about the British Royal Family—Prince William and his wife's visit to Belize?"

I caught wind of the story in the news, but I wanted to hear his perspective. "Yes, I briefly heard about the Royals' visit to Belize," I replied, "but please, tell me more about it."

His tone was animated, his pride unmistakable, "My friend, you see, we have our land. We grow cacao. We have a huge cacao plantation here in Indian Creek. The British Royal family—Prince William and his wife—wanted to come to our village, not because they like us, but because they wanted to see our cacao plantation to take it from us. We had a huge village meeting, and we, the villagers, decided to let the British Royal family know that we did not want them to come to our village."

I responded, "I read about that incident—it made headline news around the world."

I thanked him for sharing with me about these modern day challenges the Maya people face, and I felt enriched by the conversation.

He smiled and said, "It was nice chatting with you, my friend. Enjoy your visit to Lubaantun and Nim Li Punit."

As I continued on my way, the weight of the Maya gentleman's words about the Maya people's struggle with the Belizean government lingered in my thoughts. Their fight for ancestral land echoed the grievances I'd heard from Native American friends during my time on the (LCO) Lac Courte Oreilles Ojibwe reservation in Hayward, Wisconsin. My landlord, Rosanne Barber, and the Ojibwa community often spoke with sorrow about how the United States government seized their lands without compensation. He was right— colonialism morphs but never truly disappears. However, despite centuries of colonial pressure, forced removals, and economic hardship, the Lac Courte Oreilles people have maintained their traditional skills of hunting, fishing, and gathering. Their resilience is evident in their ability to adapt and survive harsh policies while preserving core elements of their identity. It is a beautiful thing to see indigenous people maintaining their culture and way of life in the face of colonial greed.

Driving through the verdant, humid landscape, my mind wandered back to the British Royal family's attempted visit. I felt a surge of admiration on hearing that the entire Maya village of Indian Creek had united to reject the Royal Family's request to land their helicopter and tour the cacao plantation. Colonialism, indeed, takes new forms, and the British Royals remain enduring symbols of that legacy. The villagers' unanimous resistance was a powerful act of self-determination and dignity.

As I gripped the steering wheel, I clenched my fist and whispered, "YES—power to the Maya people of Indian Creek for standing up against modern colonial exploitation."

The old colonial tactic of divide and conquer failed; the Maya stood united.

Arriving at the archaeological sites of Lubaantun and Nim Li Punit, I was awestruck by the grandeur and mystery of these ancient ceremonial centers. Towering stone structures, weathered by centuries of rain and sun, stood as silent witnesses to the ingenuity and resilience of the Maya civilization. I imagined the vibrant ceremonies, the echo of drums, and the wisdom of priests who once walked these grounds. The relics of antiquity—carved stelae, pyramids, and plazas—spoke volumes about a people whose culture flourished and survived against all odds.

I learned the name "Lubaantun" means "place of fallen stones" in Yucatec Maya, reflecting the site's most distinctive feature: its architecture. The structures at Lubaantun are built primarily of large black slate blocks laid without mortar—a style very unusual for Maya sites, which typically use limestone and mortar. The buildings were set on a man-made leveled ridge between two small rivers, providing a strategic location for defense and trade. The site flourished between 730 and 890 AD and was abandoned soon after. The construction at Lubaantun was a bit unusual, including rounded pyramid corners and the absence of stone structures atop pyramids, suggesting they must have used perishable materials on the pyramid tops. Lubaantun is also known for a large collection of miniature ceramic objects, thought to be charm stones or ritual items.

Nim Li Punit is about 15 km northeast of Lubaantun, set in the foothills of the Maya Mountains. The name "Nim Li Punit" comes from the Q'eqchi' Maya language and means "Big Hat," inspired by a ruler depicted with a large headdress on one of the site's stelae. Nim Li Punit was likely known as "*Kawam*" in ancient times.

Nim Li Punit flourished during the 5th–8th centuries AD and was contemporaneous with Lubaantun. It was established to take advantage of the area's natural resources and river trade networks. The site has numerous stelae, including the tallest stela in Belize, as well as the discovery of the second largest worked piece of jade in the country. While Lubaantun acted as a more administrative center, Nim Li Punit was considered more of a religious and ceremonial center. The layout and construction of the site emulate the Maya cosmological principles. I left with a profound appreciation for ancient civilizations and a fervent hope that their stories would be preserved for generations of Maya yet to come.

Southern Belize is a land of breathtaking natural beauty, with dense, emerald-green forests dominated by towering mahogany trees that form a thick, protective canopy. The air is cool and fresh, perfumed by wildflowers and the scent of rain-soaked earth. One day, while traveling toward the Guatemalan border through the village of San Antonio, I noticed a sturdy cement building with a sign reading *Maya House of Cacao*. Intrigued, I pulled over and gazed at the building's simple, yet dignified facade.

An elderly Maya man emerged, his face weathered by years of sun and work, and asked if I needed help. I assured him I was simply curious about the *Maya House of Cacao*. "Are you some kind of journalist or investigator," he asked guardedly.

I explained that I was a resident of Punta Gorda, just passing through on my way to Jalacte, and that the building had caught my eye.

He seemed to relax and began to explain, "This is where the cacao farmers in Toledo bring their cacao. From here, the farmers can sell directly to consumers in Europe and America, without any middlemen. This way, they get a fair price for their products."

As he spoke, I recalled my conversation with the Maya gentleman in Indian Creek, who had described the ongoing struggle against foreign exploitation of Maya land and resources. My admiration for the resourcefulness and unity of the indigenous Maya deepened. Their determination to protect their livelihoods and preserve their heritage in the face of outside pressures was truly inspiring.

Belize, with its population of just 400,000, is a country of astonishing natural wealth and diversity. Its pristine beaches and sparkling islands attract vacationers and researchers alike, drawn by the world-renowned marine ecosystems and the dazzling variety of tropical fruits and vegetation. The landscape of Southern Belize is a mosaic of towering mahogany, swaying coconut palms, and groves of bananas, mangos, and oranges, all thriving in the fertile soil. And the unconquerable spirit of it people matches its natural landscape.

This country is a hotspot for important biological research focused on conserving its rich biodiversity, including studies on reforestation, preserving endangered species like the Hicatee turtle and Antillean manatee, and cataloging insect and bat diversity using DNA barcoding. Marine research at Glover's Reef informs and supports coral reef conservation. Collaborative efforts with local and international partners, including wildlife forensics and genetic analysis at the Belize Zoo, make Belize a leader in research that supports both conservation and sustainable resource management. I'm proud to live in a country that takes conservation, biodiversity and climate change so seriously.

~~~~

Throughout all the years I spent living and working across Europe, and during more than two decades in the United States, I never truly acclimated to the climate and weather patterns of those places. The biting cold and relentless, bone-chilling winters of Massachusetts and Wisconsin were always a formidable adversary. Each and every year of those thirty-three years in the United States, I would count down the days until the brief, golden reprieve of summer when the sun could truly warm my bones.

My first winter in Massachusetts was a nightmare, a shock to my senses— a surreal morning when I awoke to find the world outside my window transformed, blanketed in a thick layer of snow. The landscape was dazzlingly white, silent except for the crunch of boots on ice.

Actually, quite pretty to look at from the warmth of a home, but painfully cold to travel through.

Despite my best efforts over thirty-three years in America, I never grew accustomed to the long, dark months of freezing temperatures, nor to the ritual of bundling up in endless layers of wool and fleece just to step outside.

As a warm-blooded human, my body always seemed to yearn for the sun. When I finally left the United States and made my new home in Belize, my body and spirit quickly adapted to the balmy, tropical climate—a climate strikingly similar to my homeland of Sierra Leone. In Belize, the air is thick and fragrant, filled with the scent of blooming hibiscus and the distant, salty tang of the Caribbean Sea. The heat wraps around you like a familiar embrace, and the colors of the landscape—emerald jungles, sapphire skies, and the deep, fertile brown of the earth—are a feast for the senses.

The rainy season in Southern Belize creates a spectacle of nature's abundance. Torrential downpours soak the soil, transforming the landscape into a lush, verdant paradise. The trees and undergrowth seem to pulse with new life, and the air becomes fresh and invigorating, noticeably cleaner than in other parts of the country. The rain brings a symphony of sounds: the drumming of water on broad banana leaves, the sudden chorus of frogs, and the distant rumble of thunder rolling over the Maya Mountains.

In stark contrast to my American winters—when I was swaddled in heavy coats and scarves—in Belize, my wardrobe has become wonderfully simple. Light t-shirts and shorts are my daily uniform, even during the rainy season when the thermostat registers in the high 70s. The climate is liberating, but it comes with its own set of challenges. After a heavy rain, the moist, soggy earth drives scorpions from their burrows. They scuttle up the walls of houses, seeking dry refuge, sometimes slipping into bedrooms and beds. Fortunately, the scorpions of Belize are far less dangerous than the venomous varieties I knew in Sierra Leone, where a sting could be fatal. Here, their bite is painful but rarely life-threatening.

Since my arrival in Belize in 2017, I have experienced the anxious ritual of hurricane season. Each year, meteorologists trace the swirling paths of tropical storms and hurricanes, their animated maps tracking the origins and projected landfalls. Belizeans prepare with stoic efficiency—boarding up windows, stocking supplies, and waiting for news. Southern Belizeans have often been spared a direct hit, enduring only the lashing rains and gusty winds that skirt the coast. We are often fortunate in Southern Belize, where we are somewhat protected by the landmass of Honduras that receives more wind and rainfall and sometimes helps to usher the hurricanes north towards Mexico and points north—but not always. In 2001, hurricane Iris hit landfall at Monkey River village in the Toledo District and caused quite a bit of damage. It was a small but powerful category 4 hurricane that had 145 mile per hour winds. It killed 24 people and 15,000 people were left homeless. So, when the hurricanes do hit, it can be devasting.

Every forecast reminds me of my own journey across the vast, sun-scorched Sahara Desert more than forty years ago. The Sahara is an endless wilderness, beneath a sky ablaze with heat, that many hurricanes are born. I have felt the Sahara's blistering daytime temperatures—well over 100 degrees—and its shockingly frigid nights, where the temperature plunges below zero. It is awe-inspiring to realize that the same winds that once whipped sand across my face in Africa can gather strength, cross the Atlantic, and eventually batter the shores of Central and North America.

The dry season in Belize brings its own drama. Daytime temperatures soar close to 100 degrees, and the forests crackle with heat. This is when the snakes of Belize emerge, slithering through the undergrowth in search of shade and prey. Not all are deadly—unlike the fearsome cobras and Gaboon vipers of Sierra Leone—but I still tread carefully, eyes scanning the ground for any sign of movement. My Garifuna friends, seasoned farmers, assure me that most local snakes are harmless, but old habits die hard; I never let my guard down anywhere there might be snakes. A fear of them is deeply primal—particularly for those like me, who grew up with a number of poisonous snakes nearby.

Living in the tropics, surrounded by untouched rainforest, means sharing the land with a dazzling array of insects, reptiles, and mammals. One particularly notorious insect here is the yellow doctor fly. Unlike the deadly tsetse fly of West Africa, which can cause blindness with a single bite, the yellow doctor fly of Belize is a sly, persistent adversary. It hovers with uncanny precision, targeting exposed skin—arms, legs, ankles—before landing and delivering a sharp, burning sting. By the time you feel the pain, the fly has already vanished, leaving behind a welt that swells and itches for hours. I have been stung countless times, and while the pain is fierce, my body has gradually developed a resistance. Still, I have heard of tourists and newcomers suffering severe reactions, sometimes requiring medical attention. A good insect repellent is a constant companion during the dry months.

Despite these challenges, I am endlessly grateful for Belize's climate. The warmth, the rain, the wildness of the seasons—all remind me of home, of Sierra Leone's green hills and vibrant forests. In Belize I've found a place where my body and soul are in harmony with the rhythms of nature, a place where the weather is not an enemy to be endured, but a living, breathing presence to be celebrated and respected.

~~~~

Belize is a true melting pot, ingredients blending together to create a tasty stew. When the British were preparing Belize for independence in 1981, Belize did not have the number of people to meet the requirements to form a government. As a result, people from nearby countries were brought into Belize. Other nationalities began to flock into Belize. White South Africans, White Rhodesians from present day Zimbabwe, East Indian nationals from Uganda, and Lebanese all came and settled in Belize and added to the melting pot. I found a more personal connection to Belize when I learned that the first Chief Justice of Belize, Honorable Dr. Abdulai Conteh, was a Sierra Leonean, the country of my birth.

Each ethnic group has their own unique history and contributions that have made the country what it is. One unexpected flavor comes from the East Indians that arrived here from India starting in the mid 1800's. The rich yellow spice of turmeric used in Creole jerk seasoning is a perfect example of an East Indian contribution to the unique flavors of the Caribbean. Back when Belize was called British Honduras, East Indians were uprooted by the British from their homeland around 1856. Many of the first Asians to arrive on the shores from India was a result of India's first war of independence. The British needed replacement workers, due to the fact that it became illegal to keep Africans as slaves. So, the East Indians accused of participating in the war for independence were transported to Belize to serve as indentured laborers in place of former slaves.

The second major wave of East Indians arrived from Jamaica, hired by Americans after the Civil War to work on sugar plantations mainly in the southern District of Toledo. A third group arrived in the late 19th century and early 20th century from Guatemala where they had planted coffee. They became farmers of sugar, rice, and other crops in what is now Belize.

The Jamaican and Guatemalan East Indians who came to Belize were originally indentured servants under British colonial rule. Once their contracts were completed, they came to Belize to make a better life for themselves in a place where there was more racial equity, less discrimination and more potential.

Since then, a smaller number of East Indians still immigrate to Belize from other Latin American countries—particularly people who work as merchants, educators, and professionals from other Caribbean islands that see Belize as a place with tremendous potential.

Early East Indian immigrants were predominantly Hindu, but many eventually converted to Christianity due to lack of temples and assimilation policies. The Hindi or Bhojpuri languages faded from daily community use, though some terms as well as food names survive. Traditional dances such as the *Hosay* or "who-seh-me-seh" now rarely occur, performed mainly on special occasions. Some new Hindu immigrants maintain their religious and cultural practices, but keep to smaller circles.

It became difficult for these East Indians to maintain a unique cultural identity separate from the mixing pot of Belize. Many Creoles and Mayas intermixed with the East Indians, further diluting the East Indian identity. So at this time, there are very few cultural events that maintain the East Indian identity as separate.

There are pockets of East Indians throughout Belize. Some are still focused on farming and food production, while others working in transportation are living a more urban lifestyle as officials, educators, business owners and merchants.

Many East Indians settled in Toledo, and one of them is married to my good friend, Dr. Ludwig Palacio. Curlette Ramclam Palacio is an educator and a strong advocate for East Indian culture in Belize.

Dr. Ludwig Palacio, among his many talents and achievements as a veterinarian and author, educator, is also an artist who owns the *We Art Gallery* in Punta Gorda. The lovely art in this gallery focuses on Garifuna and East Indian artists who make art focused on harmonizing body, mind, and spirit in daily life.

On one particular day, Curlette Ramclam Palacio happened to be in the gallery. An interesting conversation sparked between the two of us. I took advantage of the opportunity to inquire about East Indian culture in Belize. "What it was like growing up in Belize as an East Indian," I asked with anticipation.

She stared at me for a long moment and began, "I born in Fairview, now known as Forest Home on April 19, 1966. My early life was influenced by the East Indian traditions of that community. We live in multi-generational households: great grandparents down to newborns. Our close-knit communities take care of one another and raise their children together."

She went on to recall that her mother, Mrs. Vilma Ranguy married her father, Mr. Noel Ramclam. Her mother was a long-time educator, church leader, and community activist. She was supported by her father, who was a hard-working driver, mechanic, builder, innovator, and entrepreneur. They provided an environment that was foundational for who Curlette would become as a woman whose life mission was to retrieve and revive East Indian culture in Belize and the diaspora.

In her passion to make a difference, educated in the United States, she became the president of the southern division of the East Indian Council of Belize, an organization she helped to create to promote and maintain East Indian culture. Back in 2014, they started an important festival in Toledo called the "Yellow Ginger Festival." It is held annually in Punta Gorda in the Toledo District and it is a colorful and lively cultural event dedicated to celebrating, preserving, and sharing the heritage of the East Indian community in Belize.

Yellow ginger, also known as turmeric, is an essential staple in East Indian cooking and medicinal traditions. It represents the culinary and cultural traditions brought by their East Indian ancestors to Belize generations ago. It also represents a tangible link to the past and lends evidence of the East Indian culinary influence on today's Belizean culture.

The event provides a crucial platform for East Indian Belizeans to teach younger generations about their history, music, language, and customs. In the melting pot of Belize, festivals like this also provide exposure so that all Belizeans can learn about East Indian culture, and people of East Indian extraction can remember what is beautiful about their roots in order to preserve and honor it.

I felt incredibly honored and enriched to have this conversation with this icon of cultural preservation in Punta Gorda. Her passion and hard work are contributing to new leaders in the East Indian community, thereby passing the baton that will continue to promote East Indian culture in Belize.

Every year on September 21st, Belize's Independence Day, I watch as Belizeans from every walk of life come together in jubilant celebration, waving flags and dancing to the rhythms of Punta and Marimba. The festivities remind me of April 27th, 1961, when my homeland, Sierra Leone, gained its own independence from Great Britain. Yet, while Sierra Leone has struggled with instability and conflict since the end of colonial rule, Belize has remained blessed with peace and abundant resources, maintaining a stable government and a remarkable unity among its diverse peoples.

Belize was known as British Honduras until 1973, and was a British colony from 1862. The independence movement gained momentum in the 1950s, fueled by dissatisfaction with colonial economic policies and a growing sense of national identity. Britain's influence remains visible in Belize's political and legal systems, which are modeled on the British parliamentary and common law traditions. Britain's legacy also endures in Belize's education system, public administration, and cultural life.

No government is perfect, but Belize's cohesion stands in stark contrast to the tribalism and discord that have plagued many post-colonial African nations. As the only English-speaking country in Central America, Belize holds a unique and strategic position, poised to become a beacon of economic prosperity in the region. Its harmonious blend of cultures, resilient spirit, and breathtaking natural beauty make it a land of hope and promise for the future.

Belizeans love their land and celebrate their lives. The Garifuna celebrate their arrival on the lands on November 19th every year. The reenactment ceremony in Belize is a breathtaking, soul-stirring spectacle—a living testament to the indomitable spirit and resilience of the Garifuna people. Their story, woven through centuries of struggle and survival, stands as a powerful symbol of how diverse communities have endured, rebelled, and thrived despite the harshest conditions imposed by colonialism and slavery.

The Garifuna defied enslavement and bravely resisted British colonial domination and made a legendary, triumphant landing on the shores of Belize. Their arrival is not just a historical event, it is a celebration of perseverance, unity, and cultural pride that continues to echo through generations. The reenactment ceremony, known as "Yurumein" to the Garifuna people, is held in many towns such as Hopkins, Barranco, Punta Gorda, Georgetown, and Seine Bight. But the original landing was in the town of Dangriga. Dangriga is recognized as the principal site of the Garifuna's first permanent settlement in Belize. The reenactment ceremonies held there each year on November 19th are considered the most authentic and significant, drawing visitors from across the country and abroad.

I've had the privilege of attending several of these vibrant reenactment ceremonies and rituals in Punta Gorda, each one more exhilarating than the last. The anticipation crackles in the cool, early morning air as the town awakens. Along the shimmering coastline, a crowd gathers, hearts full of excitement, eyes fixed on the horizon. Suddenly, from the misty blue expanse, a flotilla of raft boats appear, paddled by Garifuna men and women adorned in brilliant traditional costumes. Their garments burst with color—yellows, reds, and deep blues—accented by fresh green palm leaves and twigs, symbols of renewal and hope. The rhythmic sound of drums, echoing the heartbeat of Africa and the Caribbean, grows louder as the boats draw near.

As the rafts glide onto the sand, the scene becomes electric. Those on shore step forward, arms outstretched, to welcome the new arrivals, recreating the historic moment when the Garifuna first set foot on Belizean soil. Joyful ululations, laughter, and shouts of welcome fill the air. The newly *arrived* Garifuna are embraced and together, the entire assembly surges into a jubilant procession. They march through the town, bodies wrapped in green leaves, faces alight with pride, while the hypnotic drumming intensifies. The air is thick with the scent of sea salt, sweat, and earth, mingling with the sweet aroma of coconut and cassava bread prepared for the day's festivities.

This reenactment is more than a performance—it is a sacred ritual, a communal act of remembrance and gratitude. It honors not only the Garifuna ancestors who survived exile and perilous journeys but also the enduring vitality of their culture. The celebration is punctuated by traditional songs, dances like the mesmerizing Punta and Jankunu, and heartfelt prayers offered in the Garifuna language, all underscored by the deep, resonant thrum of the drums.

Witnessing these ceremonies, I am always reminded of another great journey: the arrival of repatriated freed slaves from the Americas on the shores of Freetown, Sierra Leone—my homeland. Those freed men and women, who became the Creoles of Freetown, laid the foundations for modern education and governance in Sierra Leone, just as the Garifuna have done in Belize. Both groups, shaped by the tides of history and despite the trauma of displacement, rose to become pillars of their societies.

The parallels between the Creoles of Belize and Sierra Leone are striking. When Sierra Leone gained independence from Britain in 1961, George Price was elected the first Prime Minister of Belize and Belize City became the Capital. The Creole community in Freetown assumed leading roles as civil servants and educators, shaping the nation's future. In Belize, after independence in 1981, the Creoles of Belize City—by virtue of their close ties to British colonial administration—stepped into dominant government positions. Yet, it was the Garifuna, through sheer determination and hard work, who became the torchbearers of education in the South. They traveled tirelessly to remote villages and towns, spreading knowledge and culture, teaching in schools across the country, and nurturing the next generation.

The Garifuna reenactment ceremony is thus not only a vibrant celebration of cultural survival but also a living bridge connecting the histories of Africa, the Caribbean, and Central America. It is a day when the past and present converge in a dazzling display of music, movement, and memory—a day that leaves every participant and observer filled with awe, gratitude, and a renewed sense of belonging to a story much greater than themselves.

Chapter 9

MY JOURNEY INTO the heart of Garifuna culture began with a determined—almost stubborn—effort to learn their language. I immersed myself among my Garifuna friends and neighbors, eager to grasp the intricate rhythms and cadences of Garifuna speech. Yet, true fluency eluded me. The language was spoken mostly at home or during ceremonial gatherings, while Creole dominated daily life in Punta Gorda. I recalled how, during my years in Europe, I had picked up Italian and Greek with surprising ease—both tongues constantly swirling around me, spoken by everyone, everywhere, at all times. In contrast, Garifuna seemed to retreat into private spaces, a guarded treasure. I often wished that every Garifuna I met would address me in their ancestral tongue, but most conversations defaulted to Creole, leaving the language tantalizingly out of reach.

Despite my limited Spanish and lack of Garifuna fluency, my curiosity pushed me further. I set out to explore the Garifuna towns and villages of Guatemala and Honduras, in anticipation of the vibrant cultural exchanges that would persist across colonial borders. It fascinated me that, while Garifuna people in Belize spoke English and those in Guatemala and Honduras spoke Spanish, their shared language—Garifuna, remained a powerful bond, transcending the artificial boundaries imposed geographic borders. The Garifuna had survived centuries of displacement and marginalization, yet their language endured, a living testament to their resilience.

I boarded a ferry from Punta Gorda, crossed the Gulf of Honduras, the salt air thick with anticipation, and arrived in Livingston, a town perched on

Guatemala's northern coast and renowned as a Garifuna stronghold. At immigration, the official stamped my passport with a perfunctory nod, and soon I found myself at the front desk of the Garifuna Hotel.

The receptionist, a woman with striking features and a warm open smile, greeted me in rapid-fire Garifuna. For a moment, I felt a pang of regret—I looked the part, my dark complexion and West African features blended seamlessly with the local community, but I could only smile in reply.

Her eyes widened in surprise and when I finally responded in English, she burst into laughter, her delight infectious. With a wave of her hands, she beckoned me to sit, then called out to her daughter who appeared moments later, greeting me in flawless English.

The young woman, visiting from New York City, listened as I explained my origins—African by birth, who became an American, now retired in Punta Gorda. She told me her mother had assumed I was a Garifuna from Belize and confessed that it was very rare for someone directly from Africa to pass through Livingston.

Her comment transported me back to my early days in Europe, when I was often the only Black person in towns like Gioia Tauro, Italy, or Assini, Greece. But here, in Livingston, the town was almost entirely Black, a mosaic of Garifuna faces. What set me apart was not my skin color, but my story: I was the only African who spoke neither Spanish nor Garifuna, a curious outsider among kin.

That first night, I attended a Garifuna dance festival—a dazzling celebration of music, color, and ancestral pride. Women swirled in vibrant dresses, with geometric pattern colored like the rainbow. The men wore long sleeved shirts with capes draped over their shoulders reaching to the hem of their long pants. The air alive with the syncopated rhythms of drums, maracas, and turtle shells, instruments whose origins stretched back to across the ocean to Africa and the Caribbean Sea. I sat near the dance floor, entranced by the spectacle. When the paired dances began, a middle-aged woman, her head wrapped in a blazing red scarf, her dress immaculate and white, strode over to me. With a mischievous grin, she extended both hands, inviting me to join her. My nerves fluttered, but her insistence was irresistible—she pulled me to my feet, and together we moved to the unfamiliar beat. My own dance steps, honed in Sierra Leone, felt clumsy against the intricate rhythms, but the crowd cheered as we spun and swayed. When the music ended, she squeezed my hand, as the applause erupted. From the back row, I caught the eye of the hotel receptionist, who waved and smiled, her earlier laughter now a gesture of welcome.

After the festivities, a group of Garifuna men and women approached, speaking English, shaking my hand, and inviting me to a seaside picnic the next afternoon. Their warmth and hospitality echoed the same Garifuna tradition of communal life I'd encountered at home in Punta Gorda, where strangers are quickly folded into the fabric of the community.

By the end of my five days in Livingston, I was happy to have been immersed in the language, and I carried with me a profound respect for these Garifuna people. Their ability to maintain their African-rooted traditions, despite centuries of upheaval and the arbitrary lines drawn by colonial powers, was nothing short of remarkable. The Garifuna language, spoken across borders and generations, remained the thread that bound them together—a living archive of memory, resistance, and hope.

The wisdom of a mechanic in Ferguson, Missouri still echoes in my mind: he confidently told me that my 2003 Hyundai Elantra would run forever, thanks to its sturdy aluminum engine and parts—so long as I cared for it. He was absolutely right. Since arriving in the lush, sun-drenched landscapes of Belize, I've been meticulous about preventative maintenance, determined to keep my beloved car running smoothly. Yet, in Belize's small, scattered auto parts market, finding replacement parts for my Hyundai has proven nearly impossible. Most local shops don't stock the parts I need and ordering them from abroad means waiting weeks and paying a steep price.

My luck changed when I discovered that Puerto Cortes, a bustling, historic port city on Honduras's northern Caribbean coast, is home to a Hyundai dealership. The city itself, with its salty air and the constant hum of cargo ships, is a major shipping hub—its piers and warehouses pulsing with international trade. Through my Garifuna friends in Punta Gorda, I also learned of a vibrant Garifuna village, Travesia, just north of Puerto Cortes. The prospect of finding car parts while exploring a new Garifuna community filled me with excitement.

Having already visited Livingston, Guatemala, my appetite for adventure in Central America's Garifuna heartlands had only grown. I decided to combine necessity with discovery, planning a week-long journey to Honduras. My trip began with a ferry ride from Mango Creek in Stann Creek, Belize. The journey across turquoise waters was both exhilarating and calming, as the ferry rocked gently and the coastline receded into a hazy blue line. After clearing the formalities of Belizean and Honduran immigration, I arrived in Puerto Cortes, where the city's energy was palpable—colorful markets, the aroma of fried plantains, and the distant rhythm of Garifuna drums.

After checking into my hotel, I ventured out the next morning in search of breakfast. The restaurant I chose was cozy and filled with the warm scent of freshly brewed Honduran coffee. A short gentleman with striking grey hair approached, greeting me in Spanish.

When I replied in my halting Spanish, he immediately switched to flawless English, "Good morning, my name is Jose Escobar. Welcome to Puerto Cortes, Sir."

He handed me the menu with a gracious smile and returned a few minutes later to explain the dishes in detail.

As I finished my meal, Mr. Escobar returned, curiosity in his eyes. He noticed my passport pouch, slung conspicuously around my neck beneath my T-shirt—a classic traveler's precaution. He assumed I was from the United States, so I introduced myself, explaining that I was originally from Africa but also an American citizen, now living in Belize. He asked about my purpose in Honduras—whether I was vacationing or visiting the famous expat haven of Roatan. I told him my true mission: to connect with the Garifuna community in Travesia, just a couple of miles north of Puerto Cortes.

When I complimented Mr. Escobar on his impressive English, he pulled up a chair and began to share his story.

"My friend, I spent 14 years as a migrant farm worker in many places in the United States. I went to America to work on the farm, and I sent the money I was making on the farm to my family here in Puerto Cortes so my family could build our home. I worked on the farms in many States in the United States, and I always sent the money that I made when I worked on the farm in America to my family here in Puerto Cortes. I did not want to stay in America. I didn't want to live in America. I did not like the life over there. My living conditions were not great, and the work was very hard."

His voice carried the weight of long days and nights spent toiling in a distant land, the bittersweet ache of sacrifice for family.

He continued, reflecting candidly, "Well, there are some things that I like about America and there are many things that I don't like about America."

My curiosity piqued. I asked which States he had worked in and what kind of farm work he did. Mr. Escobar leaned back, his eyes distant with memory.

"I worked on a mink farm in Wisconsin. The owner paid us good money, but it was very hard work on the mink farm raising and taking care of those animals. I also worked in California picking cabbages and lettuce, and in Idaho on a potato farm."

Hearing him mention the mink farm in Wisconsin jolted me. My mind raced straight back to a decade earlier, when a mink farmer from Sheboygan County had come to my probation office with his Mexican migrant worker, passionately discussing the realities of migrant and farm labor. I asked Mr. Escobar if he remembered the town in Wisconsin.

He replied, "I worked on a mink farm in the town called Oostburg. My friend, working on the mink farm meant long hours, but the owner was a good man, he paid us well—very well because it was hard work."

I commended him for his perseverance and emphasized how essential migrant workers are to American agriculture.

Mr. Escobar smiled, pride in his voice. "My friend, you see I own this restaurant, and my family works here, and we have our home. I worked on the farms in America to get the money to build my home and have my business here in Puerto Cortes, so my friend, I am grateful to the United States."

His family, gathered nearby, listened intently to our exchange. I paid my bill and wished them all well, feeling a sense of kinship and admiration.

As I walked back to my hotel, I was struck by the uncanny coincidence of meeting Mr. Escobar. Oostburg, in Sheboygan County, was the very place where the mink farmer who had visited my office ran his operation. The conversation with Mr. Escobar brought back the farmer's words, still vivid after all these years.

~~~~

During my stay, I attended a lively Garifuna celebration at the central park by the seafront in the village of Travesia. The air was alive with the pulse of drums, the swirl of dancers in vibrant costumes, and the mouthwatering aroma of traditional Garifuna dishes. An older Garifuna couple, noticing that I was a newcomer, approached and introduced themselves in English. They spent years working in the United States and had returned home to retire in Travesia. Sitting with them, I listened as they recounted the rich history of their village— a community shaped by struggle, resilience, and the enduring bonds of the African diaspora. Their stories deepened my appreciation for the Garifuna people's journey and the vibrant tapestry of cultures that define Honduras.

With my mission accomplished, I purchased the much-needed parts and spare parts for my Hyundai. Even though most of my car's components were still in good condition, I decided to stock up on spark plugs and various filters and gaskets, knowing how rare these parts were in Belize. The next day, with a sense of satisfaction and gratitude, I sailed back across the sparkling Caribbean, carrying not just car parts but also unforgettable memories of connection, coincidence, and cultural discovery.

Chapter 10

AFTER BEING AWAY from Milwaukee, Wisconsin for eight years, I found myself returning by plane to Milwaukee—on my way to a Class Reunion of my late friend and benefactor Tom Johnson in Milaca, Minnesota.

The taxi driver who picked me up from the airport noticed the airline tag on luggage and said, "My friend, please be careful in this city. Milwaukee is a very dangerous city."

I asked what had happened and the cab driver in his Middle Eastern accent said, "Please whatever you do, do not go to the northside of Milwaukee, it is very dangerous, not even the police go in there. My brother was murdered on Locust Street, and his car was burnt up there, so look after yourself while you visit Milwaukee."

I resisted the urge to tell the cab driver that I was not at all a stranger to Milwaukee. In fact, I am very familiar with Locust Street because when I was a probation and parole officer in Milwaukee, most of my offenders lived on that street.

The cab driver's comments gave me an uncomfortable mixed feeling about this city that I knew so well. Regardless, I was looking forward to driving into the neighborhoods and meeting up with former work colleagues who were also retired from the Wisconsin department of corrections.

After a fitful night's sleep, I picked up my rental vehicle the next day, and I took a short drive through town. My first stop was in front of the State Office Building where Kathleen Lelinksi's office was located on the first floor. She had been such a help to me, I guess some part of me was hoping I might see her. But I was also there just to reminisce about my past. I parallel parked and inserted a quarter coin into the parking meter machine and sat in my vehicle and watched people enter and exit through the revolving doors of the State Building. As I sat and watched people entering and exiting the building, I thanked Kathleen Lelinski and felt a deep gratitude towards her for how she had helped to open the doors of opportunity for me here.

Next I drove by the Milwaukee County Jail which was located next to Milwaukee Secure Detention Center (MSDF): aka The Supermax. It houses the most violent prison bound offenders. I pulled into a parking lot and sat in my rental vehicle contemplating the jail building that I knew so well. I'd been on all of its floors. Looking at the Milwaukee County Jail to the left, I gazed at the same gate through which I used to drive to take my criminal offenders into the jail. I recalled all the times I waited before being identified by security in order to open the gate to let me through with the offender who was handcuffed and shackled in the rear of my vehicle.

To my right was the MSDF Supermax, a huge concrete cement building overlooking Interstate Highway 55 south to Chicago and north to Green Bay. I hated going into the MSDF not because of the offenders who were there, but because of the ridiculous challenge of how hard it was to pull open each door— each door requiring a supreme amount of effort because they were so heavy. There were a few sling doors, but by and large most of the doors had to be physically pulled open after security had released the electronic locks. A simple memory, but one that punctuated each entry and exit from the building.

My next stop was in the parking lot of the last State Office I worked at. I pulled into the parking lot at the Mill Road Department of Correction office and parked a good way from the building, so I could sit and watch the front door that I used to pass through. One memory after the another flashed before my eyes as I witnessed the familiar scene.

I truly enjoyed being a probation and parole agent, but an aspect of the job that I dreaded deeply was putting handcuffs on another person. I knew I had taken an oath to uphold the laws and constitution of the State of Wisconsin and the constitution of the United States, so I had agreed to do my job even though it required me to detain, arrest, handcuff and take people into custody. The idea of handcuffing terrified me because I could still remember being taken away from somewhere against my will. I suspected that my supervisor knew that I wasn't comfortable handcuffing my offenders. She likely noticed that whenever I needed to handcuff an offender, I always asked my cover agent to do the cuffing for me. Thankfully, my cover agent was a military veteran who seemed comfortable with doing the job of cuffing.

To take another person's freedom away from them brought up a conflict in me fueled by a deeper and darker imagery for me. The idea of cuffing another human being brought human trafficking to mind. While I knew that I was cuffing someone who had been convicted of a crime, I was still acutely aware that their freedom was being taken from them.

Thankfully, there were numerous aspects of the job that I liked, I was good at, and I enjoyed doing. In fact, I received praise for court documents that I wrote. As it turned out, I was good at carefully writing pre-sentence investigation reports, violation reports, situation alerts, daily logs and entries. I received numerous positive comments from various judges for my courtroom presentations, probation review reports, and in revocation proceedings. Regardless, I never became comfortable putting handcuffs on another human being, even though my job required it. It was too repulsive and immediate.

As I sat in the public parking lot in my rental vehicle still focused on the door of the building that I used to enter to go to my office, I reflected on all of the various offices that I had worked in throughout Wisconsin. For example, I was hired and began work on the south side of Milwaukee. After one year, I transferred to Hayward Sawyer County, where I spent two years in that northern office. Then I transferred to the Balsam Lake office in Region 5. After about two years, I was transferred back to Milwaukee. Then I worked in the Sheboygan office. It certainly was a lot of shuttling around, but I went where I was needed and did my job to the best of my capacity.

I was perhaps the only probation agent there who had worked in four regional offices of the Wisconsin Department of Corrections. That doesn't even count the number of times I made court presentations in revocation proceedings in adjacent counties. I was proud of my work. I managed hundreds of cases in my time there. Over time all those cases began to run together, but there are two cases in particular that have stayed with me because of the human aspect of both cases.

The one case involved an elderly man who was placed on probation for two years for assaulting his blind wife. His wife was removed from the home and placed in a nursing home. One of his court-ordered conditions prohibited him from having any contact with his wife. When his wife passed away, he violated his court order to visit the burial site of his wife. He stood about a hundred meters away and cried while his wife was being put to rest. He never had the chance to say goodbye to his wife of 45 years. My heart ached for him, despite his extremely bad choices. I knew something of the pangs of regret for not being able to say goodbye to loved ones. I was not there when my mother passed. Likewise, I wasn't able to say goodbye to Tom. I'd come to Milwaukee for this reunion in hopes of finding some closure. I thought perhaps by spending time with others who knew and loved Tom as I did it would soothe my spirit.

The other case that stuck with me seems all the more poignant now considering all the challenges currently facing American farmers and migrant farm workers in the United States and immigrants in Europe. A mink farmer came to my office along with his migrant farm worker. I went to the waiting room and brought both my client and the mink farmer into my office after they made their way through security. The farmer wanted to advocate for his farm worker, who was on probation for a misdemeanor charge and was facing deportation. The mink farmer began by saying, "Without this guy seated next to me and the two others that work for me, I would not have a mink farming business. These three workers I have are all from Mexico. They're hard workers, and mink farming is hard work. I cannot find a single American that will work on a mink farm because it's hard work that requires lots of hours."

When the farmer paused, I stated to him that I understood what he had said, and that I had compassion for the challenges he faced. Then I reiterated that I have a job to do and that is to make sure that my client does not commit another crime and he complies with his rules of supervision.

The farmer said, "I hear an accent." To which I replied that I was originally from Africa. The farmer continued, "See, I have respect for you. You came to America. You worked hard, you played it by the rules. You went to college, and now here you are, a probation officer for the State. I have tremendous respect for you, Sir."

I thanked the farmer. I was tempted to tell him my story of how I came to America, but it wouldn't have been appropriate to share something personal in the presence of a client. Still, this client brought up many personal feelings about what it is like to be an outsider who needs to belong in order to succeed and survive. Being a probation officer in this situation often left me wearing two different shoes on two different feet: on one side, an obligation and duty to uphold the law, and on the other, empathy for the plight of individuals who find themselves in a foreign country at the mercy of rules and regulations—and perhaps even facing discrimination by those who can make or break their lives.

After I sat on the parking lot lost in thought for a long while, I returned from my stream of consciousness that had led me to reflect and reminisce on my 14-year tenure as a probation and parole agent. I pulled out of the parking lot feeling complete with the rattling of the skeletons in the closet of my memory. In that instant, I felt a pang of longing to return back home to Belize.

Soon I came to a four-way intersection with stop lights on Wisconsin Avenue. As I waited at the red light to turn green, two vehicles came from behind me and passed me in the right lane at a high speed and blew through the red lights. Within minutes, I heard multiple gunshots and multiple police cruisers arriving at the scene. I drove to my hotel recalling what the Middle Eastern cab driver from the airport told me about how dangerous Milwaukee had become. There had always been crime in Milwaukee but not the level it had grown to. I drove through the streets and neighborhoods where I used to make home visits to my offender clients and found most of the homes boarded up and garbage strewn all over. All things change, but it made me sad that things had gone so far downhill in this area. I made it back to the hotel to prepare for the long drive to Milaca, Minnesota the following morning.

Chapter 11

I ONLY HEARD about Tom's death after his funeral and I always had tremendous regret that I wasn't able to be at his funeral. How could I not have been there after he had done so much to help me? It was one of the things that haunted me most after I left the United States. Try as I might to shift it, it left me with an incomplete feeling that I couldn't resolve within myself, even after I had paid several visits to the cemetery to pay my respects. I hoped that this trip was an opportunity to finally have some sort of closure after so many years.

I was looking forward to meeting all of his classmates at their class reunion. The class reunion was an opportunity to meet not only his classmates, but to also meet two of his best friends for the first time. I was terribly curious because Tom had talked about one of them in particular quite a lot. To finally get to meet this gentleman was like reaching a handshake back in time and getting to make friends with the cast of characters I had only heard about, creating another opportunity to know the man who changed my life.

I left Milwaukee early in the morning for Milaca, Minnesota which was a six hour drive. After being away from Milwaukee for over seven years, I was eager to drive on the same highways I had driven on numerous times in the past when I was a probation and parole agent. The traffic from Milwaukee to Madison was heavy, as was expected in the early morning hours. Though after merging on Interstate 95 north towards Eau Claire, the highway became wider, and traffic flowed more swiftly. I made stops in the small cities and towns in the counties that I previously worked in. The city of Rice Lake in Barron County was a city that was inhabited predominantly by white folks, though I noticed a change in the demographics of the population with a little more of a racial mix showing up than there used to be.

When I arrived in Milaca, before even checking into my hotel, I drove straight to the cemetery to pay my respects. I stood at the gravesite of my friend and benefactor. I closed my eyes and reflected on that hot day in Sierra Leone that I met him, just a child trying to make a few coins to help feed my family by selling oranges. He saw me that day, and it changed my life.

I thanked him and asked for forgiveness for not being present at his funeral. I left the cemetery, a weight lifted from my shoulders—relief that I had that moment to speak to my friend. For some reason, I truly felt he heard me and forgave me. I felt a sense of sweet relief pour through me as a tear came to my eye. It felt like grace.

Through the years I met all of Tom's family members, but I never met any of his friends. It was like a missing puzzle piece that held information I didn't know. For some reason, he rarely talked about them. He only told me about one of them, though he didn't even include his friend's name in those reminiscences.

Social media is an amazing connective mechanism. I'd received a Facebook friend request from a Lonnie Strandlund followed by a message that said, "Hi Francis, my name is Lonnie, I was one of Tom's friends in high school and beyond. I heard you are coming to the reunion. I hope to see you there."

I was delighted to hear from Tom's friend and became eager to meet him at the reunion.

In the morning before the reunion started, I was invited to breakfast by Gary Grant and his wife, Joy. Gary was the gentleman who told me about the reunion coming up. He was a friend of Tom's elder brother Doug Johnson. I met Gary and Joy at a restaurant. It was a delight to meet Gary and Joy in such a lovely interaction. Like Tom, Gary was a military veteran who fought in the Vietnam war. After breakfast Gary drove me to the Milaca war memorial to pay our respects, and we took a few pictures there together.

I finally showed up at the Milaca Golf Club where I knew everybody was expectantly awaiting my arrival—the mystery man from Africa they had heard about, but never met. I entered the club and waved to the small crowd waiting there and took a seat at the counter where I ordered a glass of water.

As I took my glass of water and walked outside, a short gentleman also came outside, approached me and introduced himself saying, "Hi Francis, I'm Mike Soderlund, one of Tom's friends." We shook hands and hugged, feeling a deep camaraderie, because of our shared appreciation of our friend Tom. We again shook hands and hugged while everyone watched. Mike and I took a seat. I was beaming with delight and happiness to finally meet Tom's friend. I finally figured out that he was the friend Tom told me about some years ago in Sierra Leone. I was finally able to put the puzzle pieces together to figure it out, despite the fact that the only thing I knew was that each time Tom went home to Minnesota, he would visit his friend and his wife in their home and that his friend and his wife played music—mystery solved.

While Mike and I sat and chatted, we were joined by three of Tom's other classmates at the table and a photographer took our picture, a wonderful moment captured in time. After our picture was taken, they left and we continued our conversation. Mike shared details with me about his relationship with Tom, their time spent together, and the things they did together as friends whenever Tom came home from his flying jobs in Africa and Europe. I was delighted to finally meet Tom's close friends. These people had known him from high school until death. They had history. For me, it was one thing to meet and know Tom's family. It was another thing and a big deal to actually meet Tom's best friend. Being one of the most important people in my life, I've always had tremendous curiosity and a desire to understand and know the man more deeply because of his profound consideration for me.

The reunion began. Everyone sat and after a brief speech, the moderator said, "Today, we have a special guest."

Much to my surprise, I was handed the microphone and asked to say a few words. Even though I had never met these people, I immediately felt a strong connection and bond with them because of our shared connection to Tom. I felt the presence of Tom's spirit among his fellow classmates. It was not only a class reunion, but a spiritual communion of sorts as well.

"Good afternoon everybody, my name is Francis Mandewah. Some of you may have already heard about me. If it wasn't for one of your classmates, Tom Johnson, who is not here today, I would not be here speaking to you. Your classmate Tom Johnson was a remarkable man who transformed my life from poverty and physical abuse, and war and famine in Africa to the experiences of freedom and opportunity of America. I came from a dirt-poor African family and background with little hope or prospects. I had no choice but to drop out of school because my poor family could no longer afford to pay my school fees. I miraculously met your classmate Tom Johnson while selling oranges. Out of his tremendous goodwill and generosity, he voluntarily chose to give me support for an education. He brought me to America and paid for my college tuition, room and board. Back when he tragically passed away in Africa and his body was flown here, I was not able to attend his funeral and that has haunted me ever since. Even though I had met his family, his mother and brothers, I felt incomplete. Meeting you all today, his classmates and friends—and particularly you Mike Sonderlund, has been a huge relief and a big deal for me."

My heart welled up as I felt an incredible sense of gratitude flow through me on that stage. I paused as the whole crowd clapped. I sensed that they also were touched by the sincere affection and gratitude I felt for our shared friend. I told them about the book that I wrote that chronicled my relationship with Tom. I'm sure they all felt incredibly curious about it but also happy to know a person so special to them had been memorialized for his good works in the world.

At the end of my presentation, I was given a present of a hand-knitted blanket, which I still have to this day. It provides me with a kind of warmth that supersedes the physical. It provides warmth of the heart through the living bonds of friendship that gives life true value.

Mike and I talked the evening away. I asked him what it was like for him to hang out with Tom when they were younger. He told me a story from the summer of 1983. He tilted his head back and cupped his chin with his right hand. He suddenly gave his forehead a tap with the palm of his right hand. "Yes," he exclaimed. "I remember. This was quite the adventure. We almost died!"

"Forgive me if I misremember some of the details. It's been 30 years," Mike said. As he set the scene a small crowd formed around us.

The Alaskan Highway lay bare before them. The summer August sun was on high. They rode with the windows of the 1969 Dodge seafoam green station wagon down, letting the hot air hit them in blurry waves as they intermittently mopped the sweat from their brows. Willie Nelson's "Stardust" was playing on the portable cassette player. Mike noticed that the pits of Tom's faded blue t-shirt were soaked through. The sweat from his neck had turned the color of his t-shirt from a pale denim to a navy tone. Upon recognition of the heat's effect on the driver, Mike reached for the thermos lying between them on the bench seat of the car. He carefully removed the aluminum cup from the top and unscrewed the lid.

"Hey Buddy, you need some water. You're going to sweat to death."

The two chuckled as Mike filled the cup with iced water from the thermos. Mike tapped Tom on the arm with the full cup saying, "Here." Tom smiled and took the cup. Tom gulped the water down. It was like manna from heaven. Condensation formed on Tom's sunglasses, so he removed them. Tom swore the sun felt the relief of the cold water and lowered its temperature just a smidgen.

"Can you drive," Tom said to Mike.

"Sure. I napped through Saskatchewan. Pull over."

"OK. Let's stop at the next gas station."

They didn't need gas yet, but Tom was cautious and didn't want to pull over on the side of the road on a stretch of two-lane highway.

"How many miles have we covered?"

"Odometer says we're 900 miles in."

That was under half of the distance they had to cover. They'd set out on the 7-day trip on Saturday morning. They'd drive all day and camp at night. Alaskan highway #1 was a long stretch of Interstate that connected the United States to Canada. The map they were following traced a clear, though jagged at some points, line from Minnesota to the Yukon territory. Tom had come up with the idea to go digging for gold in the Yukon territory after working in Canada and flying his boss into the "bush" for weekend gold panning trips, where they'd found flakes of gold and a ¼ ounce nugget.

Mike spotted a sign: "Weigh Station. Rest area 5 miles." He turned to Tom and said, "That's as good a place as any."

"Sure," Tom said.

Tom used his left hand to guide the steering wheel and reached for his sunglasses with his right hand. He used his knee to hold the wheel steady while he wiped the lens with the bottom of his t-shirt. Mike used his left hand as a visor over his eyes trying to bring the road back into focus, battling the sun's dazzling light bouncing off of the asphalt. "Oh. Look," Mike pointed at a red circular sign in the distance. It was a Petro station off the side of the highway.

"That's great. But how do we get over there," Tom retorted.

"Good question."

It turned out that the rest area/weigh station was just before an exit. Tom carefully guided the Dodge station wagon along the off ramp and merged onto the service road leading to the major roadway. As they pulled into the gas station, Mike began to feel hunger pangs. He had $100.00 cash, earmarked for gas.

When he told his wife about the trip, she was happy enough, and, as she tended to do, she lent her full support to his efforts. She was the one who'd fixed up the thermos of ice water. She also prepared a cooler filled with sandwiches and snacks for the trip and carefully packed the cargo area with camping gear. He had everything he needed to make it to Canada without incurring expenses outside of gasoline. There was no need to buy food. She'd even packed carrot sticks, banana bread, jerky, and chips.

Tom pulled into the gas station and aimed the passenger side toward the pump. He exited the vehicle in slow motion, using the side of the car to pull himself to standing. He stretched his arms high above his head and let out a sigh of relief. Mike was bent over at the time, stretching his back and legs at the time of Tom's exhale. The sound gave Mike a jolt. "You alright there, old man?" Mike chuckled.

"Well, Sonny, I'll tell you. I sure could use a bathroom," Mike said in a high-pitched impersonation of a stereotypical old geezer.

Just then the attendant appeared out of nowhere. Mike and Tom looked at one another, exchanging a knowing look. "How did this guy sneak up on us," they asked one another silently.

"Regular or premium?" the ghostly figure asked.

"Regular," Tom responded. "Hey. Where's your can," he added, stepping side to side to signify that it was a bit urgent that he find it.

The attendant's skin looked greyish, even in the tawny sunlight. He was a wisp of a man, middle-aged. He took a break from unscrewing the gas cap on the station wagon to lift his scrawny arm and point a thin finger to the side of the building. Tom's eyes followed the trajectory of the finger. Tom nodded and his feet instinctively began in that direction.

By the time Mike stopped watching Tom walk away the attendant had inserted the nozzle into the tank. The man stared intently at the ground. "What was so interesting," Mike wondered.

"You out here all alone? It's awfully quiet," Mike's awkward attempt at a conversation starter.

After a long, awkward pause the attendant said, "Yep," without raising his eyes.

Mike watched the numbers flip on the gas pump. One gallon…two… three. Before long, Tom came around the corner wiping his hands on the front of his jeans.

"You know, Francis, this was in 1983 and gas was only around $1.25 per gallon back then. What I wouldn't give for prices like that now. So, anyway, I didn't have to use the can, but I figured I should go before we got back on the road. Funny the things you remember," Mike said to me before going on.

"No paper towels," Tom called out after him.

Mike waved his hand in the air to acknowledge Tom's words.

The bathroom was less than pristine but not altogether disgusting. There was both a urinal and a commode. Mike was grateful not to need the commode. There was a dirty bar of blue and white soap on the edge of the sink. Mike looked around as if he might find an alternative source of cleanser hiding in plain sight. After giving up, he hesitantly took the soap in one hand and turned the faucet with the other. The water came out with a strong, cold gush. He suddenly understood why the soap had dirty fingerprints on it. He, too, left the bathroom wiping his hands down the front of his clothes.

"$24.00," the attendant said to Tom as Mike was approaching the car. In that moment Mike considered buying a candy bar, but just then a wave of hot wind swept his face, and he could picture the chocolate melting before he could even have a chance to enjoy it. It was high noon. Mike rounded the car and opened the rear cargo door to access the cooler. He grabbed some sustenance and climbed into the driver's seat while Tom paid the attendant.

Back on the road, Tom whistled and commented on how surreal the gas station experience had been. "Right," Mike said. "That guy was really creepy. I wonder if he's like that all the time."

"He might be a zombie by day and a vampire by night. Good thing it's broad daylight!" Tom said with a chuckle. Tom unfolded the map and traced their path. He concluded that they were about 250 miles away from the Banff Jasper National Park and the campgrounds where they would hold up for the night.

"Nothing but space and opportunity," Mike said biting into his ham sandwich. "I can do it in four and a half hours."

"You won't mind me sleeping."

The station wagon pulled into a round-about parking area just beyond a sign that said "camping grounds this way" around 6:00. They'd gotten stuck behind an 18-wheeler, and what was supposed to be a 4-hour sprint, turned into a 6-hour crawl. The two men parked in line with the other vehicles and began to gather their gear. The two were loaded down with backpacks and sleeping bags. They followed the uphill trail, dotted with signage to reach the campgrounds. After hiking for 20 minutes, they reached a clearing in front of a densely wooded area.

"This must be it," Tom said. "We can set up camp just beyond those trees. Let's take advantage of this last bit of sunlight to start a fire."

"The temperature is dropping fast," Mike complained

"We'll want to be able to see. Plus, it'll get colder in the middle of the night."

Setting up camp went without a snag. Tom sat down in front of the fire and finally ate while Mike changed his shirt. The two agreed to bed down early so they could get an early start. The sky was the darkest of blues, dotted with stars. All the constellations shown. Mike couldn't sleep. He lay there staring at the stars, breathing the forest air. The smell of pines, wood-lily, and wild roses dancing in his nostrils. Mike lay listening to the cicadas, trying to will himself to sleep.

Mike said he must have fallen asleep because the next thing he knew there were glimmers of sunlight, and Tom was shaking him awake but signaling for him to keep quiet. Tom's face was close to his, and he was motioning upwards with his hand. Mike followed his silent directions and rose to his feet. Tom led Mike by the arm, away from their camp site into the trees. Just as the two stepped behind a tree, Mike heard a hoarse roar. It was a bear. Tom held his index finger in front of his lips and gestured to the path they'd taken to get to the campsite. The bear had begun to ravage their little campsite. The sleeping bags were tattered. The cooler was turned over and the bear was feasting on its contents. When the two had exited the trees immediately surrounding the clearing, they took off running as fast as they could. They didn't stop running until they reached the car.

Out of breath, Mike said, "Holy Moly. That was close. How did you know?"

"I woke up and couldn't go back to sleep. I was hunting for firewood, so I could make coffee when I saw him. He wasn't that big, but still…he was a bear."

"Well, thanks for coming back for me."

Tom tapped Mike on the arm and said, "I'd like to think you would've come back for me, too." They laughed.

Mike had never had an encounter with a bear before. He asked Tom, "what do we do now?"

Tom hunched his shoulders and casually said, "We wait. He'll go away."

"There goes breakfast," Mike sulked.

Tom patted his front pants pockets, then his rear, finally his t-shirt. He hung his head low and finally sighed, "The keys. The keys are in the side of my backpack." He sat on the rear bumper of the car, bent over, and rested his head in his hand, his sweaty blonde hair hanging loosely between his fingers as he shook his head.

Mike joined him on the bumper of the station wagon. "No worries. We'll just wait until the bear leaves and go get them."

"Right."

Tom and Mike took turns pacing with arms folded across their bodies for the next hour. "Do you think it's been long enough?" Mike half directed his question to the open air.

Tom responded, "Probably. Let's go check."

The two made their way back up the wooded path, across the clearing and into the tree line, cautiously. Tom stopped abruptly when they caught sight of their ruined camp site. He raised a hand signally to Mike to stop. They scanned the area for the bear. Nothing. They breathed deeply and entered the area. They quickly began to gather the remnants of their belongings. Tom found his backpack intact. Mike was not so lucky. The bear had torn his into several pieces. Tom's sleeping bag was unrecognizable as was the cooler. Mike bent down to retrieve the thermos and had to stifle a scream. He began to walk backwards in slow, deliberate steps until he bumped into Tom.

"Hey," Tom said.

"Shhhhh," Mike said, tapping Tom's leg and pointing. The bear was back.

Tom grabbed Mike by the arm and led him backwards into the wooded area. The bear had caught sight of them and had begun to advance. Mike was on the verge of panicking and gestured to start running. Tom grabbed him by the arm and whispered, "not yet." Tom took the thermos from Mike's hand and took aim at a tree behind the bear. He let the thermos fly. The sound of it landing attracted the bear's attention and the two of them took off running through the wooded area. They quickly found the path and ran all the way down the trail, not stopping until they reached the car. Tom frantically searched for the car keys in the backpack and high tailed it out of the parking lot. Panting, they rode in silence.

They drove for just over an hour and Mike finally broke the silence. "Where'd you learn how to handle bears? They got bears in Africa?"

Tom rolled his eyes. "You know what they have in Africa? Coffee. And I want some."

Mike laughed. He found a stick of jerky on the front seat and offered Tom half. A wave of calm had begun to settle in on the two of them, and suddenly the car began to lose momentum followed by a jolt and a cloud of smoke coming out of the front of the car. Tom pulled to the right.

Tom brought the car to a stop and traced the silhouette of the steering wheel with the palms of his hands before slamming it. He rested his forehead at the top of the steering wheel for just a moment. Mike said, "It might just be the radiator. You've got some antifreeze right?"

They got out of the car to inspect the damage. The engine was too hot to check the radiator. Besides with the hood up there was no longer smoke. Tom opened the cargo area and lifted the storage area cover to unveil the spare tire but no antifreeze. "Well, alrighty then," Mike said.

Tom was visibly frustrated. Mike assured him that they would be alright. They just needed to assess the situation, and they'd figure it out. Mike leaned over the engine and told Tom to try and turn the engine over. He could not. "See if the radio works." It did.

"I wonder," Mike said scratching his head. "Old clunker like this? I bet it's the fuel pump."

"Well, that's just great," Tom said. "Now would be a time to pray for an angel."

"Surely someone will come along."

"We can definitely hope."

They sat there until 8:00 a.m. before there were any signs of life. An 18-wheeler whizzed by. That was no help. Then about an hour later, a lovely pair by the name of Steve and Marion from Ontario pulled over to see what the matter was. There was an auto parts store about 15 miles down the highway.

"Can we get a ride into town?" Tom's eyes were hopeful.

"Sure we can take you into town."

"Thank you."

Marion offered them water and bologna sandwiches. They accepted gratefully. The couple chatted them up on the way to the auto parts store. When they arrived in town, Steve and Marion said their goodbyes, wishing them good luck.

"Well, at least we're not starving to death," Tom said with a smile, "Now we just need to find a way back."

"Your mood just picked up."

"Well, a good bologna sandwich will do that to you. Ya know?" Tom chuckled. Besides, Steve and Marion are just proof that you are right: help is on the way. It was 11:00 a.m.

They sat there for another hours, camped out in front of the auto parts store watching nothing but 18 wheelers pass by, waiting for someone going West back in the direction of their abandoned vehicle. A farmer named Ned in a well-worn, white pick-up truck pulled up on the pair and asked where they were headed. Tom let Mike do the talking.

"Our wagon broke down a ways back. I have a fuel pump I need to put on. Need a ride back."

Ned surveyed the situation and said, "Well, Fellas, I've got good news, and I've got bad news. Good news is I'm headed West. Bad news is I only have room for one of you." He pointed to his full truck bed.

Mike and Tom looked at one another, incredulous. Tom spoke first saying, "You go. I don't know how to do the work anyway. You go ahead. Get us ready to go and I'll catch up."

Mike tried to offer Ned a $10 bill, but he refused to take it, saying "my pleasure, neighbor," with a wave. It was 5:00 p.m. by the time the two left.

Mike climbed into the passenger side of Ned's truck and settled in for the 25 minute ride back to the station wagon. As soon as Mike approached the car a wave of nausea overcame him. He kicked the dirt. Tom had not given him the keys to the car. He could not believe their luck. How could this be happening?

Mike sat on the rear bumper of the station wagon to wait. An hour went by and only two more cars passed and neither of them stopped. As the sun began to set Mike decided he had to do something. It could take Tom all night to find someone willing to give him a ride. What could he do? Mike had a bright idea. He walked around to the front of the car and grabbed ahold to the car antenna. He bent and twisted it every which way until it came off the car. He took the broken antenna to the car window and fished it into the side of the rubber seal of the window. After a considerable amount of effort, he was able to get the door open. "Eureka!" he said to the open air.

The sunset was upon him. He unlocked the back door, fished out the flashlight, climbed into the cargo area, got the tools, then popped the hood and assessed the situation. He says he can't remember exactly how he got it done, but by midnight the fuel pump was installed. Hopeful, yet worried, he settled in to wait for Tom. It had been hours. Mike took a clean shirt from Tom's backpack and lay down in the cargo area. The carpet on the floor of the cargo area was itchy and smelled of oil and gasoline from years of use. He propped his head up on his arms and breathed through his mouth to avoid the smell.

At around 2a.m. Mike awoke to the sound of tapping on the glass. Mike raised his head and caught sight of a Royal Canadian Mounted Police officer. "Good morning. You been here all night?"

Mike struggled to bring the world into focus. He sat up on his elbows and said, "Yes, Sir," in a groggy voice.

"Looks like your friend has come to the rescue. Let's get you going. He says he's got the keys, but it looks like you got inside."

"Yeah, I worked it out," Mike retorted.

Mike pulled his legs under himself and made his way out of the passenger side door. He stretched and yawned feeling surprisingly well rested. For the first time in over 24 hours he had thoughts of where they were headed. He remembered. Prospecting for gold. This could be it. Finally. It. He was reinvigorated and determined to get this problem solved. With the officer holding a flashlight on the engine, Tom put the key in the engine, turned the key, and the engine roared to life. All three of them let out a happy yelp of "Oh! Yeah!" When the work was done the officer packed up his wares and bid them adieu, pulling off into the darkness.

"Ready?"

"How about that coffee?" Mike said.

Mike asked Tom if he should do the driving because he'd had a nap and Tom had been waiting for a ride in the heat all day. Tom agreed and said that the officer told him about an all night café about another 15 miles past Jasper where the auto parts store was. They would stop there.

As promised, the café appeared in the distance with flickering neon lights to the right of the highway. The seafoam green station wagon pulled into the lot and easily parked right in front. The two made their way inside, sat in a booth and had coffee and eggs. The midnight sustenance of champions. They decided that they both needed some shut-eye before they got back on the road. They went back to the car and agreed to pull to the edge of the parking lot, away from the entrance and sleep in the back of the car. Tom turned on the hazard lights so that none of the 18 wheelers would back into them.

After about 4-5 hours of sleep the two awoke to the sun's glaring beams. Tom turned the key in the ignition of the Dodge and got nothing in response, just silence. "What? What's the matter?" Mike asked.

Once again Tom traced the silhouette of the steering wheel with the palms of his hands before slamming his palms into it and placing his forehead on the steering wheel. "I left the hazard lights on all night. I didn't want anyone to run into us in the dark. It must've drained the battery."

"It's your turn to pray."

This time help didn't take long. Around 7:00 a.m. a man named Sam came to their rescue. Sam had it all. He turned his truck around to face the station wagon and quickly hooked up the jumper cables. Mike told him about the bear and the hodge podge of would-be rescuers who didn't quite have everything they needed and the ultimate goal of their adventure. Sam smiled and offered each Mike and Tom a Coca-Cola from his cooler.

"Thank you for your kindness, Brother. We've been stranded out here in this 80 degree heat for over 24 hours. I really appreciate your help. Let us pay you for your trouble," Tom said to Sam.

"No. No. You just be sure to help another friend in need when you can. That's how you pay me back."

"God truly works through people, and I thank God for you today, Sam. You saved us," Tom said shaking Sam's right hand with his left hand resting on Sam's shoulder.

Tom took the wheel and eased onto the two-lane highway in the opposite direction of Sam. "He sure was a nice guy," Mike commented. After driving for about an hour, Mike commented, "And I'm starving again."

"I second that. We need to find food and check the map. I think we still have four more days of driving left."

"The rest of that trip was smooth sailing, Francis. We made it to the Yukon territory within eight days total, despite having been attacked by a bear and stranded on the side of the road, left to starve for a day," Mike relayed.

"So, did you strike gold, or no?" I asked.

"Not much. Ours is a story of hope and adventure. Not of striking it rich. Don't look at me like that. My wife was disappointed, too. Especially when I came back with a story, no gold and no cooler or sleeping bag." He went on to tell me how Tom was one of the best friends he ever made, that their trips to the Yukon were fodder for he and Tom's conversations for years, and he wouldn't trade those experiences for anything.

We had a hearty laugh. In that moment I felt close to Tom. This memory that Mike shared with me was one of the type of man I knew Tom to be. He was kind and brave. Grateful and faithful. This was my closure. This was a celebration of his life. I was grateful for the opportunity to have met and talked with Mike, and I told him as much. We parted company, promising to keep in touch.

Something else from the reunion stuck with me. Lonnie Strandlund wasn't there. Mike told me that he couldn't attend because of Covid. I was very much looking forward to meeting Lonnie. Even though he couldn't make it to that event, I was determined to meet him. The next day before I was to leave

Minnesota, I drove to the town of Mora where Lonnie lived and met with him in a parking lot at a gas station. I was delighted to meet another of Tom's friends. Lonnie shared the memories of times he and Tom spent together. He told me about a road trip he and Tom took to Florida in a Chevy Camaro. The two of them rented a place and the police broke into the rental looking for someone else. He said it was scarry in the moment, but they had a good laugh about it after the fact. "Look out for the police," became a running joke between them. Lonnie was a delightful man, and talking with him gave me an even fuller picture of Tom.

I needed to say goodbye to my friend by paying respects at the cemetery one last time. I drove slowly, somberly through downtown Milaca, traveling along the remembered streets of my friend and benefactor's hometown.

I stopped in front of a two-story building that displayed the sign: "First National Bank of Milaca," Tom's bank. My breath caught in my throat. All the checks he wrote and sent to me in Sierra Leone were all drawn from the First National Bank of Milaca. Every check, a Godsend and the fulfillment of a promise that Tom made to me. Each time I received a check, I would meticulously examine every detail, from the inscription on the check to his signature, his address, and the name of the bank. I imagined that if I were to go inside the bank and say my name to the man who ran the bank, Pete Allen, who was a leader in the banking industry, he would remember my name because of the sheer volume of checks that came through and cleared.

I drove past what was once Tom's home, now occupied by a different owner. I remembered the time I spent in that house visiting with Tom's mother, Virginia. It was in that house I first met Tom's children, Ivanna and Kenneth, there to visit their grandmother. It was in that house that I met Virginia's brother, Dr. Wilson Pond, and his wife, Masha Pond. It was in that house that Virginia told me about her Presbyterian Missionary grandparents who migrated from Connecticut and built the first church in Minneapolis. The house will forever remain in my memory.

Just as I was about to merge onto the Interstate towards Wisconsin, a county sheriff officer parked in the middle of the divided highway stuck his head out of his cruiser window and called my name, "Francis!" and waved to me. I wasn't sure, but I suspected that he was a relative of one of Tom's and a resident of Milaca. I continued to drive, reflecting on how meaningful it was to have made so many connections in Tom's hometown.

I arrived in the town of Hayward late in the evening, drove through town, passing by the State of Wisconsin office where I worked as probation and parole officer. I checked into the hotel at the Lac Courte Oreilles Casino Lodge on the reservation. I had mixed feelings about being back in Hayward after almost ten years. On one hand, I was truly excited and looked forward to connecting with the Native American friends who came to my aid and welcomed me into their close-knit community. On the other hand, there were still memories of the trauma of my negative experiences with the Department of Probation and Parole.

Much like my newfound Garifuna family in Belize, the Ojibwe Chippewa saw me for who I intended to be in this world. The profound kinship was heartening. These familiar feelings reverberated through me as I drove through Hayward to the Casino Lodge.

I recalled the saying Tom Johnson said so often, "God always works through people."

I do not entirely know how God works through people who judge and persecute unfairly, but at the very least, adversity has taught me that light and mercy can be found even in the darkest of times. Adversity has taught me to stay true to my faith, even in circumstances that seem impossible.

When I first arrived in Hayward, I encountered substantial barriers when it came to finding a place to live. The town of Hayward, primarily settled and inhabited by Caucasians, proved unwelcoming; no one would agree to rent me an apartment. Time after time, I faced polite rejections or outright refusals. It was a disheartening and isolating experience.

Rosanne Barber, a respected member of the Native American Ojibwe Chippewa reservation, approached me and said, "You can stay in the house behind mine. It's yours for as long as you need." Her gesture provided not only a safe place to reside but also a sense of belonging, my first signal that the Native American community would accept me as one of their own.

The Native American Ojibwe Chippewa were the people who came to my aid when I didn't know anyone. The community helped me not feel alone when I was a stranger in a new town. The Ojibwe were the ones who spoke out against the injustice I faced and endured at the hands of my supervisors during the darker days of my time at the Department of Corrections.

I still remember my lonely days in Milwaukee. It was hard to make friends at work or in the larger community. There were only five staff in the Hayward office, made up of three probation and parole officers and two secretaries. No matter the temperature outside, it always felt emotionally cold inside the office.

There were times when I would walk into the office and say, "Good morning!" Often, none of my coworkers would respond. Most of the time they would not even look at me. The atmosphere was unnerving. The air would go from an eerily quiet to the constant slamming of doors. I often felt my work environment was deliberately made hostile. My supervisor went as far as to accuse me of illegal activities after I was the victim of an internet scam. This accusation was ran all the way up the flag pole to the District Attorney's office.

When news began to spread among the Native American community in Hayward that I had been wrongfully charged—and wrongfully prosecuted—for crimes that both the District Attorney's office and the Hayward Police Department knew, or certainly should have known, that I did not commit, my Native American friends rallied to my side without hesitation. Moved by the knowledge that I was innocent, and armed with the direct, compelling evidence showing I was the victim of an internet scam, they felt it was their responsibility to act. On the day of my court appearance, a group of my Ojibwe friends showed up at the courthouse in protest, their presence a clear statement against the injustice I was facing.

I still remember that moment—standing outside the courthouse, feeling the weight of fear and anxiety pressing down on me. Suddenly, I saw a small crowd gathering—all friends from the local Ojibwe community.

One of them, Michael Littlefeather, walked up and put his hand on my shoulder. "We're here for you," he said, his voice steady. "What's happening to you is wrong, and we want everyone to see that you are not alone."

The Native Americans in Hayward were the visible forces that were behind me, who protected me and came to my aid when I was being treated unjustly. But I found another resource in the unlikely form of a practical self-help guide titled *Live and be Free Through Psycho- Cybernetics* by Maxwell Maltz, M.D., F.I.C.S.

I came upon it in the used books section in a thrift store in Hayward. This book armed me with practical psychological tools and skills perfectly suited for that time in my life. The book guided me and taught me how to protect myself while working in a hostile environment with colleagues and coworkers who were unkind to me.

The well-worn copy I stumbled upon made an unanticipated difference, teaching me coping skills that I was grateful for then and continue to practice until this day. There are many vital psychological and practical aspects of the book. Page 72, in particular, talks about *Psychological Relaxation* which puts me in a proactive mindset. The keys are as follows:

1) FORGIVE YOURSELF

2) FORGIVE OTHERS

3) KEEP UP WITH YOURSELF (NOT OTHERS)

4) SEE YOURSELF AT YOUR BEST

There are also affirmations given in the book that give practical psychological tools and skills. These exercises became my sanctuary, my safety, and created a peaceful mental fox hole:

- My thinking and my attitude are calm and cheerful.
- I act and feel friendly towards other people.
- I am tolerant of other people, their shortcomings and mistakes, and I view their actions with the most favorable understanding possible.
- I will not allow my judgment or attitude to be affected by negativism or pessimism.
- I try to smile as often as possible; at least several times a day.
- I respond in a calm and intelligent manner without alarm, no matter what the situation.
- If I cannot control a situation, I always try to react in a positive manner, even to negative facts.

I found out that responding in a calm and intelligent manner without alarm, no matter the situation, was the most effective skill and tool I could have. My mindset gave me the mental strength and discipline to withstand, respond, and react with dignity to the negativity that was thrown at me by coworkers and supervisors. They did everything they could to make me lose my temper and blow up on the job, but they did not succeed. They didn't realize this little used book had given me the tools and the skills to effectively react and not respond in kind to the aggression they were bombarding me with. I had secret protection in the form of psychological strategies that worked.

When I had to interact with any of them. I used the psychological tools and skills that I had learned and internalized, and my response was less than satisfying to them, because they couldn't knock me off my center. I was determined to protect my peace.

The tides began to shift a bit when I was having lunch at the Hayward Cooperative Diner one afternoon, and a gentleman walked up to my table and introduced himself saying, "Hello, my name is Kris Melberry, I am the County Executive of Sawyer County. Are you one of the Probation and Parole agents here in the Hayward Office?"

I confirmed, and Kris shook my hand and said, "Welcome, we are happy to have you in Hayward."

Kris joined me at the table and a conversation ensued while we ate our lunch. On another lunchtime occasion at the Hayward Diner, he actually arranged to meet, sat, and had lunch together. A conversation ensued. I told him about myself: from Africa, went to school in Massachusetts, now a United States citizen and working for the Wisconsin Department of Corrections. I found Kris to be friendly, and he showed genuine interest in me. He referred to me as a friend, and He told his wife about me, his new friend, and she suggested inviting me over for a visit to their home.

When Kris heard about the injustice I was facing in the Hayward office, he spoke out against the unequal treatment I was enduring and denounced the supervisor. I recall Kris said to me, "Francis, if I was still the District Attorney of Sawyer County, I would have thrown out all the bogus charges that were brought against you in court." Kris, was an attorney, and at different points in time had been elected Mayor of the town of Hayward, and as the County Executive for Sawyer County.

Kris's empathy for me is a testament that there are good people and not so good people in all cultures. I met two other men, Chuck and Waldo, who also had strong feelings about equality and justice in addition to being genuinely interested in getting to know me. I came to consider Kris, Waldo and Chuck to be true friends.

The support from the Ojibwe Chippewa community was more than just a moral gesture; it was an act of solidarity rooted in shared history and empathy. The Native Americans in Hayward, having experienced discrimination and injustice themselves, understood intimately what it felt like to be seen as an outsider and treated unfairly. They identified with my struggle and felt a powerful obligation to come to my aid.

The support I received reached all the way to tribal leadership. When Mr. Luis Taylor, the Chairman of the Ojibwe Tribal Council, learned that I was not only facing wrongful prosecution but also enduring a series of blatantly unequal, disparate, and unfair employment practices, he decided to act on my behalf. Mr. Taylor called me into his office one afternoon and explained, "We're not going to let this go unanswered. What's happening to you can't continue."

True to his word, Chairman Taylor drafted an official letter addressed directly to Governor Jim Doyle. In this letter, he boldly stated, "This man is being targeted because of his race and national origin. I am asking you, Governor, to see that these unequal and unfair practices end. Fairness and justice should not be denied to anybody in our community."

Rosanne later told me, "We know what oppression feels like. You're facing injustice, and when we see that, it's our duty to help. We won't just stand by."

The Native Americans' willingness to offer me a home, speak on my behalf to State officials, and ultimately stand beside me in court, left a profound impact on me. It was solidarity born of empathy and shared experience—a bond formed out of mutual understanding of struggle and a deep sense of what is right and just. Through their actions and words, they made it clear that, in the face of injustice, I was not alone, and their sense of community became a lifeline during some of my hardest days.

Chapter 12

I REMINISCED ABOUT the good times ice fishing and the powwows in addition to the community resources that helped me to survive despite terrible circumstances. The morning before I left, I was excited to see my Ojibwe friend, Rose Barber, for breakfast at a restaurant I used to frequent with her when I was her tenant. Our special bond was enduring, and it was as if no time had passed.

As much as I was excited to see Rose again after eight years, she too, was eager to learn about my contacts with the Maya Indians in Southern Belize. Despite the distance, many Native Americans feel a kinship for the many indigenous peoples in the Americas and have a curiosity about the history, hardships and triumphs of other tribes. Not only do they share a deep love of the land and a profound relationship to it, they also share the scars caused by colonialism and a fervent desire for justice, autonomy and better times for all. Growing up in Africa in a community that also suffered from colonialism, I feel a kinship of shared experience as well.

Rose wanted to know more about the Maya people and their practices. During the two years I lived in Hayward, I attended several powwows, tobacco ceremonies and rituals. I told her I noticed some striking similarities between the cultural traditions of the Ojibwe Chippewa people and the Maya of Southern Belize.

One of the most fundamental is a deep respect for Mother Nature and the environment—a shared thread that runs through both cultures. Both also have important ceremonial dances. Among the Ojibwe, powwow dancers wear colorful regalia of feathers, beads and quills, crafted and cared for with great dedication. They tap their feet and move in circles, each dancing alone but together—a dance of Spirit.

The Maya of Southern Belize perform the Deer Dance, which involves characters such as deer, jaguars, monkeys, Spaniards, an elderly couple, hunters and sometimes a loyal dog. Performers wear elaborate, symbolic masks and ceremonial clothing, all treated with deep reverence.

While the Ojibwe drummers sit in circles and beat a single drum together like shared thunder while chanting their sacred songs, the Maya Deer Dance music is more elaborate, made up of mahogany marimbas being struck in unison and conch shells blown like trumpets. Rattles and flutes are played along with murmurous chanting while drums pound out the heartbeat of the forest, both tribal dances, honoring their sacred relationship to the Earth and its creatures.

I also shared with her other similarities that I saw: the tobacco ceremony of the Ojibwe has a similarity to the gifting rituals the Maya perform at their sacred sites. Both perform these rituals and dances in their villages and sacred sites, creating a continuity over the eons. Both the Ojibwe and Maya dances and rituals not only have their unique ceremonial significance, but they also serve as a form of resistance and cultural preservation in the face of colonization and modern pressures. Culture matters.

Rose was intrigued by my cultural relativism experience between the Belizean Maya and the Ojibwe customs and traditional practices. It shows the thread of human experience, and how it weaves us all together.

It was wonderful to see her again, and to reflect on both memory and culture with her. The beauty of true friends that become old friends, time is relative, eight years is but the blink of an eye. We chatted about ceremony and culture and colors and smoke as if we'd seen each other the day before. Such a blessing.

Chapter 13

I HAD ONE last person that I felt I needed to spend time with in order to offer a sense of completion on this visit to the United States. I did not know her very well, but she was precious to me, nonetheless. Sometimes small actions make a big difference in a person's life, having huge repercussions in the best of ways. She did that for me. Linda Roesler was a co-worker and my immediate supervisor who acknowledged and supported me when others didn't. She stood for justice when others wouldn't. It was a real gift, even though it arose naturally and without provocation from her instincts and ethics.

I had a number of supervisors when I worked throughout the State Offices in Wisconsin: Milwaukee County, Sawyer County, Ashland County, Douglas County, Polk County, Rusk County, Sheboygan County, all during my tenure at the Wisconsin Department of Corrections.

The only Supervisor that was in my corner was Linda. She was like Kris Melberry and not at all prejudiced against because of my national origin. She didn't treat me like a color. She treated me like a person. She saw what the State was doing to me, and though she didn't verbalize her disdain, her body language clearly spoke of the fact that she empathized with me. Witnessing what I had been subjected to, she sympathized with me about the injustice and wrongness of that treatment.

During the time I was wrongly accused, I went through a process where I was under investigation. This period was incredibly stressful. The supervisors knew what was going on when HR sent investigatory notices to me. Other supervisors just handed me the investigatory notices and scurried out the door without a backward glance, avoiding any real interaction. They acted as if nothing that mattered had just occurred. When Linda was the one who got the request from HR to serve one of these investigatory notices, she entered my office with full knowledge and regret for how it would land for me.

She gently laid the sealed envelope on the desk in front of me and said, "Francis, they told me to give this to you."

She stood in front of me in my office and closed her eyes and paused for a moment while maintaining presence. When she opened her eyes, she shook her head with consternation and tightened her lip, expressively saying with her face what she could not say with her mouth. However, it was all the eloquence I needed to feel supported. She left quietly, but her presence stayed with me. I didn't feel alone in a lonely place. Linda was a compassionate supervisor. She made a hard time easier for me. For that, I respect and appreciate her.

Contemplating those fraught times and her support during them, I drove that last mile into Milwaukee to meet with Linda and another co-worker, her own son Nick Roesler.

We met at a restaurant and banquet hall in Wauwatosa, Wisconsin, which is a metropolitan area in a western suburb of Milwaukee. It was a place we both knew and liked: home-made food with an unbeatable fish fry. As I entered the door, I saw Linda and Nick sitting at a table. She flashed a broad smile at me and waved. Before I knew it, we were walking down memory lane together, reminiscing about the past—both the good and the bad. I once again thanked her for her support in a time when I was being treated like an outsider.

Years ago Linda gave me a beautiful mug adorned with cherry blossoms. When I set off on my journey to Belize, I carefully packed the mug up and carried it to my new home because it was precious to me. It contained memories I wanted to keep. I let her know that it was still in my possession, and I remembered her fondly when I used it. She gave it to me without a thought, years ago, just because I liked it. Such a generous person!

Continuing on with her natural way of being, she insisted on paying for my lunch, and would not take no for an answer. I drove away with a smile. It gave me a lift to see her after all these years, a supervisor turned friend who was allied to my cause.

Epilogue

AS IS LIFE, all good things must come to an end, and I had reached that moment in my sojourn back to the United States with no regrets. I was excited to go back to my life in Belize, a place that was once strange and far away, but now was as familiar as an old friend. Once upon a time, the United States was my big dream, my highest aspiration in life. The United States had held the dreams of my youth, the promise of a life filled with opportunity. Now, I'd moved on to new dreams, turned the page to a new chapter. Belize is my home now, my place of promise.

After packing up my belongings and driving to return my rental car. My first flight from Wisconsin to Houston went off without a hitch. After an easy flight with little turbulence, I landed in Houston, Texas which is one of the main hubs in the United States for international travel to Central America and the Caribbean.

United Airlines: Flight 1569 announced the boarding of my flight. I made my way toward the boarding tunnel, took my seat and settled in for the next leg of my journey.

I was pleased it wasn't a full flight and was almost gleeful that I had three seats to myself in my row. It was going to be a nice flight!

I looked to the row adjacent to me, and I couldn't believe what I saw. Could it be?

That sure did look like the Prime Minister of Belize. I wasn't sure whether to trust my eyes or not, but then I heard a person say to him. "Hello, Prime Minister Johnny Briceño, I'm a businessman in San Pedro."

Well, that confirmed it. I wasn't seeing things after all—it really was him.

I waited until the flight took off and people began to move about the cabin. I moved to the aisle seat in my row nearer to him to introduce myself.

I said, "Hello Prime Minister, it is an honor to meet you. May I please speak to you for a minute?" He was so personable he actually moved and sat next to me so we could speak more freely.

After three decades of service, PM Johnny Briceño is known for his grounded, pragmatic leadership and his ability to bridge diverse communities in Belize. He has a reputation for empathetic and hands-on governance. Under his watch his political party emphasized social investment, inclusion, and national unity rooted in broad local support, administrative experience, and a vision for inclusive national development.

I imagined that he was the perfect person to talk to about my film project because of his deep understanding of immigration and migration as well as of the importance of racial harmony and cultural awareness.

I told him that I am a friend of Hon. Mike Espat, and I am now a permanent resident of Belize. I have moved to Punta Gorda to retire. Originally, I was from Sierra Leone before moving to the United States to complete my education and work. Since that time, I have written a memoir about my adventures, and I am working on turning that story of endurance, faith and friendship into a film.

After explaining to him more fully about the important and relevant themes covered in this adventure story, he expressed interest in my project, which lit me up with joy and hope. We discussed the possibility that some of the Sierra Leone shots could actually be filmed in Belize in the village of Barranco, since there are places in the landscape that look so similar. He told me to keep his office informed of my progress. I expressed my gratitude to him for listening and giving me feedback about my project.

As I settled back in to take in the final hours of my journey, I felt a smile inside me. Not only was I going home, but I was going home to a place where I felt honored, and that my presence had value. I was going home to a place not where I originated from, but to a place where I knew I belonged.

If you liked,
The Road to Belonging: My Journey to Punta Gorda, Belize,
check out the author's first book:

Available at most Internet book retailers!